Africa: Birthright and Calling

Helen Vanstone

Onwards and Upwards Publishers

3 Radfords Turf, Cranbrook, Exeter,
EX5 7DX, United Kingdom.
www.onwardsandupwards.org

This first edition published in the United Kingdom by Onwards and Upwards Publishers (2017).

ISBN: 978-1-78815-661-5
Typeface: Sabon LT
Photography: Janet Parrella-Van Den Berg (p.4)
                 Helen Vanstone (other photographs)
Graphic design: LM Graphic Design

Printed in the United Kingdom.

The author and publisher gratefully acknowledge the permission granted to reproduce the copyright material in this book.

Every effort has been made to trace copyright holders and to obtain their permission for the use of copyright material. The publisher apologizes for any omissions or errors in this regard and would be grateful if notified of any corrections that should be incorporated into future reprints or editions of this book.

Endorsements

In my role leading a development charity, I saw and heard first-hand the impact Holly made in Uganda. The overwhelming sense is one of respect and love, born out of genuine partnership where she modelled those qualities herself. Holly understands the true nature of mission.

Andy Read
Former CEO, Links International

If you are planning a short/long term trip to a developing country, I recommend you read this book. With humour and honesty, Holly shares the fun, challenges and diversity of living in Uganda. She understands and embraces the African way of life, always respecting and honouring their values and traditions.

Be challenged to step out of your own comfort zone.

Samuel Kibuule
Ugandan health worker, living in the UK

Not only is depression still greatly misunderstood by many, but some Christians feel that they can exempt themselves from its shadowy touch by pushing themselves to greater commitment and personal sacrifice. But as she writes with raw honesty and candour, Holly shows that heroes of the faith achieve great things, not because they don't experience seasons of gloom, but because they endeavour to be faithful through those times. Highly recommended.

Jeff Lucas
Author, speaker, broadcaster

About the Author

Helen trained as a primary school teacher near Liverpool, returning to her Surrey roots to begin her first teaching job. Alongside class teaching, she was responsible for music throughout the school. As her career developed, she moved into managerial positions, culminating in headship of a junior school.

A personal crisis led Helen to consider leaving the UK to fulfil her ambition to live and work in Africa. In 2005 she moved to Uganda to help establish a primary school, where she remained for eight years. Since returning to the UK, Helen has continued to visit Uganda annually to provide both teacher and leadership/management training.

To contact the author, please write to:

Helen Vanstone
c/o Onwards and Upwards Publishers
3 Radfords Turf
Exeter
EX5 7DX

Or send an email to:

hvwellspring@yahoo.co.uk

Dedicated to Phil and Anne, my
church leaders and great friends,
who believed in and encouraged
my African adventure always.

Contents

Author's Note

The names of some individuals in the book have been changed to protect their identity.

At birth, the name chosen for me was Helen. This is the name by which I am known professionally and by my family. Over forty years ago, a large group of friends began to call me Holly. This has continued and I was known as Miss Holly whilst I was the head teacher of Wellspring School in Uganda.

ACKNOWLEDGEMENT

I am so grateful for the help and support Mary Stuart gave me in the editing and proof-reading process. Her meticulous attention to detail was invaluable and very much appreciated.

I am grateful also to Luke Jeffery, managing director of Onwards and Upwards, publisher of my book, whose communication over the months has been very helpful and supportive.

Preface

For twenty-five years Mike and Beryl Godward were the leaders of a church in Thurrock, Essex. Their work led them on mission trips to Africa where they helped support various development and outreach projects. During one visit, they were taken to view a plot for sale in a place called Bweyogerere, situated 9 kilometres east of the capital of Uganda, Kampala. The area was a coffee plantation and could be reached only via a mud track, so there were few houses or businesses at that time. There and then they made a decision to buy the land and use it for a new vision and purpose. The following year, work began to construct a centre which would provide many benefits for the local community.

Moving out to live in Bweyogerere in 1995, the Wellspring centre being almost complete, Mike and Beryl set about establishing the various facets of the ministry, building links with local people to attempt to meet some of their needs. This included a venue for church meetings, a conference hall, a health centre and also accommodation for students participating in the leadership training programme which commenced later that year. At the beginning of 2000, a nursery school was established with eight pupils attending on the first day.

The Wellspring work and team expanded as new initiatives were developed, such as loan schemes for micro-business development, housing projects, a dental surgery and modular training for local pastors and leaders. The aim throughout was to provide holistic programmes to meet the needs of local people. The mission of Wellspring has always been: Grow a People, Develop a Community, Transform a Nation.

In December 2008, Mike and Beryl moved to live and work in South Africa and the mantle of Wellspring leadership was passed to Herbert and Eve Wanjala. They are the current directors, working hard to maintain the excellence that Mike and Beryl encouraged and fostered in every aspect of the work. Under Herbert and Eve's leadership, developments include an International Secondary School, community physiotherapy, training in dressmaking, hairdressing and jewellery-making and the regular clearing of rubbish and waste from the surrounding area. Wellspring is registered as a Non-Governmental Organisation and as such it has been recognised and given credit by both local and national governmental bodies.

Alongside its work in Uganda, similar projects have been established in both Kenya and Tanzania. Over the years many church teams from the United Kingdom, America, Europe and several African nations have spent time at Wellspring to offer support through practical help, leadership training, youth and children's work and medical assistance. This support has strengthened and encouraged the team at Wellspring as it seeks to make a positive difference in this corner of our world.

Foreword

Holly Vanstone is a remarkable woman. We spent seven years working together in Wellspring, Africa. To say the school and education programme went up a gear would be an understatement. Today it is a model shaped by Holly's commitment, sacrifice and utter dedication over those years.

Holly, we salute you.

Mike and Beryl Godward
Founders of Wellspring

Prologue

You are a missionary woman.

You will be going abroad helping and changing schools.

Other schools will ask for assistance and you will be moving on to help these too.

You will also be training head teachers as well as working alongside women.

You will continue to do this into your old age.

You will live a long life.

This prophetic word was given to me nearly twenty years before I became head teacher at Wellspring School in Uganda. At the time, I had no idea how this prophecy could be fulfilled. I had always held a strong connection and love for Africa and felt that somehow these words were linked to this passion. The following account demonstrates how God worked in my life to transform this prophecy into my destiny.

PART ONE

Road Map

The road up and the road down are one and the same.

Heraclitus

Jinja Road.

Send Me

'What is she up to now? Call her back inside. She's embarrassing us all!'

I was outside on our garage driveway, where I had set up a table display of toys and games, having decided to sell some of my own well-loved items to neighbours and people walking past our house that day. I attracted their attention and cash when I explained my reason and motivation.

As a family, we were very involved with a local church and my father was one of its leaders. He had arranged for a missionary from Africa to tell our church about the situation they were facing. What horrified me was hearing about children and adults in their village having no food, because their harvest had been so poor that year. He explained how they were affected by sickness and disease, with many dying from starvation. We heard names like Elijah, Grace, John, Martha – friends he loved and lived alongside.

Until that day I had never considered anyone not having food in front of them each day. At first, I began slipping food from my own plate into a plastic bag hidden on my lap. After several attempts, I understood that these potatoes, sausages and cakes could not be sent anywhere other than the bin. The toy shop on the drive was my next plan. I was serious: something had to be done.

Several years later, television news was informing us that 1,000 children every day were starving to death. It seemed that famine was being used intentionally as a war weapon in the Civil War of Nigeria. It was 1968, and as a teenager now, I found more productive ways of responding to this humanitarian crisis: I became a local volunteer for Oxfam which worked as part of the international relief effort to get food, medicines and help to Biafra. Many years later, my parents told me they hid their newspapers at the time as the pictures of the suffering upset me so much.

In *Strength to Love,*[1] Martin Luther King explained the difference between pity and compassion. Pity will empathise only, but compassion moves you to take action.

When I was selling my toys, I was moved on behalf of individuals I had never met but I knew their names. They had become real people to me, not simply informed statistics. There was no other response possible for me other than acting on their behalf. At the age of seven my heart was connecting with 'family' in Africa. Over forty years on, I would act in a far more significant way to reach my 'brothers'.

I have written my story, not to highlight myself, but to illustrate how God sets hopes and dreams in our hearts from a young age and remains faithful to them. We can make choices and decisions that lead us through difficulties and far away from our potential calling and destiny. God, however, does not pause at our diversions: he weaves all of life's paths into the road he has intended for us.

---

[1] *Strength to Love;* Martin Luther King Jr. (1963)

World View

As young children, we loved it when our aunt and uncle returned on 'furlough' from China and Malaysia. Uncle Stanley was rather mysterious. He wore thick-rimmed glasses, had pure white hair and referred to Auntie Norah as 'Mum'. Both of them were devoted to the people of China where, since the 1930s, they had been working as missionaries.

The Chinese loved visual stories, so Stanley would set up a stand on a street corner, use pictures on a flannelgraph board and explain the story of God's love for humankind. With the Chinese language being pictorial, this method of communication was easily understood. Suffering extreme circumstances, temperatures, dangers and even the death of two children during those years of service, their zeal and passion never diminished. They spent their whole lives helping the Chinese at the cost of their own family life, as my cousins Christopher and Faith were separated from them for extremely long periods whilst attending boarding schools in England.

We heard about long treks across mountain tracks by mule cart, serious fevers and health problems, deeply superstitious and antagonistic villagers, and yet Uncle Stanley remained cheerful and positive, always totally committed to his work in which Auntie Norah worked patiently and faithfully alongside him.

Through hearing from our relatives as well as other frequent visitors to our home, a world outside of our comfortable Surrey lifestyle was opened up before our eyes and ears. Gladys Aylward, a legend of that time, visited us and relayed how she had trekked across the mountains with over a hundred children as they escaped from Japanese invaders. Her story was later portrayed in a film, *The Inn of Sixth Happiness,* starring Audrey Hepburn. Another frequent visitor was a leader of a large gypsy tribe who had had many escapes from knife-wielding attacks in opposition to the gospel message he shared as he travelled across Europe. A lovely couple, a Moroccan man Amar and his Canadian wife Jeanne, had to flee a very dangerous situation and were left homeless. We offered them our home and they stayed several months for their baby to be born in safety. They arrived with nothing and we enjoyed discovering fantastic bargains that appeared miraculously in local shops just as they were needed. I spent many hours playing piano duets with Jeanne, who had the largest hands and span I had ever seen!

Many Sundays, our parents hosted the Sunday speaker in our home for lunch and tea before the evening service. We had to be very polite and considerate. We were not to eat our food too fast and finish before him. The guest would always talk a lot so we were left pushing a last potato around our plates, willing him to eat up and finish so we could all move onto pudding. A 'look' from our mother definitely kept that potato moving. I felt most indignant when one visitor commented on the variety of cakes provided when so many went hungry in the world. We scowled at each other in response, knowing that our mother had cut back on our weekday menu in order to provide these treats. He didn't hesitate in eating several pieces, so at the time we decided he couldn't have been too concerned for the hungry!

Other Sundays, a youth team would be with us and my older sisters eyed up the good-looking men who amused and teased us throughout the day. On those occasions, all five of the females in the family stood around our large kitchen table, buttering and spreading three or four loaves of bread to make into sandwiches. Home-made cakes included ginger cake, scones, sponges, fairy cakes, fruit cake and flapjacks. Even now, flapjacks are known to be my frequent contribution when cake is required. I taught my Ugandan friends how to make them when I lived there.

Looking back, our home was always open to neighbours, friends and people in need and we received many worldwide travellers as our guests. We grew up being taught that what we had, which was actually little, could be shared with others. We felt connected to a far bigger world outside of our immediate environment. To this day, my three sisters and I are involved in local and global initiatives that help people in need and provide opportunities for them to find friendship and engage with their local community.

Fully Immersed

At the age of fourteen, I was baptised by full immersion. This is a symbolic and public ceremony that is usually carried out in evangelistic or community-based churches. On this occasion, ten young people – all members of our church – were getting baptised. The girls wore dresses made of towelling. This of course soaks up the water, making it very heavy, which is not helpful when you try to exit the baptismal pool. At the front of our church, there was an area where the floorboards opened up to reveal a baptismal pool beneath. The water was always heated, but as this occasion was held on a cold January evening, we shivered with cold and nervousness as we stepped down into the pool. Over the years, I had enjoyed just watching this spectacle but now it was actually my turn. Two church leaders stand either side of you, gripping your hands as they lean you backwards and you go completely under the water. You resurface, catching your breath, and then aim to move gracefully towards the side steps, the thick towelling dress working against you. Each dress had weights in the hem to keep the garment down in a dignified way as you stood in the water. My weights, I discovered, were missing and the dress floated around me. I felt like a large lily pad on display.

The significance of all this is to show publicly that you have made a commitment to be a follower of Jesus and you choose to lay down your own agenda to follow his example and teaching. As each person rose up from the pool, the congregation sang a short song which they had selected. I had chosen one inspired by the words found in Isaiah 6:8:

> *Mine are the hands to do the work*
> *My feet shall run for thee*
> *My lips shall sound the glorious news*
> *Lord, here am I, send me.[2]*

---

[2] Dr Howard W Guinness (1903-1979); established the Inter-Varsity Fellowship.

At this point in my life, aged fourteen, I wasn't imagining being sent anywhere far from home. Seeds were being sown though, even at this early age. It would be another forty years before those seeds would burst fully into life.

Signposts

When I left school, I trained as a primary school teacher in Ormskirk, near Liverpool. During the spring of 1973, I had interviews for a teaching post. Having been accepted by Surrey, I was free to make my own individual applications to schools. I had applied for a specific post in Woking, Surrey. The evening before I travelled for an interview there, I received a telegram from my mother. It transpired that a head teacher had visited the Surrey Education Offices and had read my details. She wanted me to attend an interview at her school. As I was travelling down to London the following day, I agreed I would visit her school first. It seemed the perfect job for me and I did not hesitate when she offered it.

She allowed me to use her phone to contact the Woking school and explain that I had accepted a post and would no longer need to attend their interview later that day. To my amazement, a very apologetic secretary told me that there had been a mistake. There had been a post advertised but it was now no longer available. I had therefore travelled from Liverpool to London for a phantom position. This had, however, led me to visit a school I had known nothing about but where I now had a job.

It was very obvious that something or someone was working on my behalf. I recalled a recent prayer I had prayed, that God would direct me to a school where I would feel happy and confident. I had seen an image in my mind of a signpost showing I would be in a ten-mile radius of Guildford. Several months later, when I had settled into my job and a new home in Cobham, I noticed a signpost outside the post office. It showed 'Guildford 10 Miles'.

At the time of my initial prayer I was not choosing to live a particularly godly lifestyle and really it was rather impertinent of me to ask God for help and direction. However, I felt I had been graciously gathered up and planted in the right place. It was here I discovered a rather radical Christian group that was having a lot of influence on the surrounding area and across the country and in 1974 I became a member of that group, known then as Cobham Christian Fellowship.

These were early pioneering days in churches where the structures and expressions of church were being transformed in new and dynamic ways. I look back on my twelve years as a member of this group with fond memories, knowing that many roots of Christian teaching and living were established in me there.

During the eighties, I followed a church leadership course for a year. One section was entitled, 'Salvation Landscape'. This took us through the history of the early missionary movement, large evangelistic crusades, the house-group movement, church planting and other postmodern church developments. It became clear to me that such influences had changed the course of my family's life and mine: my father was brought up initially in India where his father, my grandfather, was a captain in the army. As an adult, my father came to faith after the war at a large Tom Rees crusade in London and his sister, Auntie Norah, with her husband Stanley, served as long-time missionaries in China. For my part, I had been a member of the pioneering church in Cobham which led the way during the seventies' house-group movement. From there I had moved with a small group to Molesey to establish a new church in that area. I could recognise clearly a thread running through this genealogy that linked us all to an expression of mission in some form. This recognition felt like a 'kairos' (watershed) moment and I knew God had something significant for me to fulfil in the future.

I recalled the story of Abraham, and how God told him to leave his country and his family. God explained that Abraham had been blessed in order to *be* a blessing. This resonated with me. I felt greatly blessed in many ways but knew there was a far greater purpose to be revealed in using that blessing for the benefit of others. It felt as if a seed in my heart was germinating and I was willing to nurture that seed in order for it to flourish and bear fruit at the right time.

My professional teaching career really developed following my move from Cobham to Molesey. I began a new job in the local school, where very soon I was promoted to a senior post, followed by the role of deputy head teacher and then finally acting head teacher. A short while later I was asked by the diocese of Guildford to take up an acting headship in a school in Send. Following my time there, I took up a post as head of a school in Surbiton, under the Royal Borough of Kingston. I really loved being in a managerial role, leading and working with a team of staff.

Driving to school one day, I was taken by surprise. It seemed God was showing me that I was a square peg in a round hole. This was not how I felt at the time and I was finding my work extremely rewarding. Two years later though, I was very unwell with severe depression brought about by pressure and stress. When I first arrived at the school, I realized there were political challenges I had not been made aware of which would make my work more challenging than I had anticipated. In a pressured situation it can be too easy to excuse yourself from facing the important issues because you are busy dealing with the urgent. And so it was with me: I had neglected some areas that I should have dealt with and consequently the school had not achieved its potential, as revealed in our Ofsted report around this time. I took advice from my union and decided to resign.

During this time, while I was off sick, my mother died suddenly. I had lost my good reputation, my job, my career and my second dearly-loved parent. Her very last words to me had been an expression of her trust and belief in both God and me. Although I knew she was very concerned about how I would earn my living once I became well again, she reminded me that God had a calling on my life and that all things would fall into place. A trustworthy promise from Proverbs 3:5-6 had always helped my parents through severe difficulties:

> *Trust in the LORD with all your heart and lean not on your own understanding.*
>
> *In all your ways acknowledge him, and he will direct your paths.*

When you experience a crisis, such words of promise and assurance can be hard to grasp. Feeling you are at the 'end of the road', a way forward seems impossible. Depression can seem like a dark, deep pit. The mind is no longer capable of imagining any hope on the horizon. Unless help is given and received, such hopelessness can result in tragedy. If we believe God stays with us throughout these crises, then we can believe and know he will take us through them and into a hopeful future.

'You can't get there from here!' will never be the response God gives us when we look to him for direction. Although I was at my lowest ebb and facing a dead end in my work and career, I clung on to the promise my parents treasured and never doubted God's love and faithfulness to me, even though I had no idea how the future would map out from there.

Again, God gathered me up and led me into a new sphere of employment. I ran some music workshops for local pre-school children and did supply teaching in several schools in the area.

During one term's supply teaching, I saw an advertisement for a music post in a school in Epsom. I got the job and began two days a week teaching music with every class from nursery through to Year 6. This was challenging but huge fun. Many of the pupils had very tough home situations and many struggled academically. A particular highlight was a series of African drumming workshops I organised for the older pupils. Their performance a few weeks later was enjoyed and celebrated by the whole school. The experience of success, creativity and working together in harmony had united and motivated this usually disruptive and belligerent group. I was so happy in this work but after two years there, I was planning to move on to something new.

Goal Setting

On 1st January 2005, I had sat down and written myself a set of goals for the coming year. I had done this for several years, grouping my goals under health, exercise, interests, finances, challenges and travel plans. This would help motivate me and focus my attention on specific activities and make it easy to monitor my achievements as the year progressed. That year, one of my goals was to explore opportunities to do a season of voluntary work in Africa.

I had visited Africa briefly on two occasions, once to Ethiopia and once to Tanzania. I contacted a friend, the director of the Christian charity Links International. He was very enthusiastic and assured me that I would be welcomed by many of the organisations he worked with and knew well. Consequently, I was put in touch with Mike and Beryl Godward who headed up an NGO in Uganda called Wellspring. They had urgent need of a head teacher for their primary school. In between my first and second interview with them, I looked at Wellspring's website to learn more about their work. As the first page opened up in front of me, I saw a verse right at the top. This was a verse I had underlined in my Bible twenty years earlier, as I knew it referred to a connection between myself and Africa. It read:

> The LORD will always guide you and protect you in a sun-scorched land.
> You will be like a garden that has plenty of water, like a spring that never runs dry.
>
> Isaiah 58:11

This organisation had the hot sun of the tropics and the spring (or well) – hence the name Wellspring.

I had no doubt that this was where I would soon be heading, and shortly afterwards I was invited to be the head teacher at Wellspring. This was an unpaid position and they wanted me to commit to the role for two years beginning that October, which I agreed to do. It had been only six months since my January goal-setting, yet now all was settled for my new adventure into Africa.

I wrote down my thoughts the day I heard I would be going. This was 6th June 2005:

I know now my future. It will be two years living in Uganda – until I am 55, help! What or who will I be then, I can't imagine. That's the hard test because I can't actually imagine any of it: the school way of operating, the kind of people I will meet, living next to Mike and Beryl, away from everyone here. A long way away. It feels scary suddenly and I wasn't expecting that.

Little did I know that my two-year commitment would extend to eight! I wonder what my journal would have said had I known?

Africa: Birthright and Calling

PART TWO

Heading Out

Education is the most powerful tool which you can use to change the world.[3]

Nelson Mandela

Leading up to the Nelson Mandela stadium for a Wellspring sports day.

---

[3] Address by Nelson Mandela at the launch of Mindset Network, Johannesburg, 16th July 2003

Finally There

'Show me your ticket, Holly, before we go for a coffee.' I was at the airport ready to fly to Uganda. The previous three months had been hectic, as I prepared my house for renting to tenants – this would be my income whilst in Africa – sorted all my possessions, wrote a will, had health and medical requirements arranged, sold my car and said final farewells to family and close friends. In all this busyness I had got the flight time wrong! I was informed that the last call had gone out and that I would need to run straight away if I wanted to be aboard that flight. Now in tears, I gave a hasty hug to friends and moved quickly. Sadly, my sisters arrived at the time I had given them but too late to say goodbye to me.

Soon, I was up and away into the sky, feeling more positive and settling back into the long flight ahead. I remembered a verse from Psalm 121. My father had been in the RAF during the war. When he would be out bombing enemy planes, his mother had encouraged him with this particular promise:

The LORD will watch over your coming and going.

Psalm 121:8

I decided this was a promise I could rely on also and that God would guard my coming and going always.

As we began the descent nearly nine hours later, I caught my first glimpse of Uganda below. It was very early morning and a soft grey haze with pink tints hung across Lake Victoria. Just before landing, I could see three ladies walking in a line along a dirt path that ran parallel to the runway. They were carrying bundles of long sticks on their heads and took slow, graceful steps. The whole scene felt peaceful and serene. The image seemed so different from the hustle and bustle I had left behind in Heathrow Airport. I felt welcomed by these three ladies who moved alongside me as I looked eagerly through my small window, anxious now to be off the plane and on Ugandan soil.

Once I was through immigration and had retrieved my case, I searched in the crowd for Mike and Beryl. They were easy to spot amongst all the local people; everyone smiling and waving in welcome to someone they were meeting. Mike drove us to Kampala where I was astounded by all the traffic, hooting, dust and noise that enveloped us. Shops lined the roadsides with wares spreading out onto the pavements. There seemed to be people everywhere, walking purposefully towards a destination. Motorbikes cut in between the traffic or edged along the inside of our car at traffic lights. Hawkers knocked on our windows to encourage us to view and buy their goods. As it was still early morning, everyone was heading to work or school. I saw one woman carrying her suitcase on her head and others carrying baskets of bananas to sell. I particularly noticed school children who looked very smart in their clean, brightly-coloured uniforms. Those who saw me smiled or waved which felt very welcoming.

Finally, we turned off the busy main road into the road where Mike and Beryl lived. Mike hooted his horn and eventually the huge gates were unlocked and we drove into a large compound with tall exotic plants all around it. I was shown the house I would be renting which was large and airy, despite the rising temperature outside. I knew I could easily create a comfortable home here once I had put out some of my pictures and small items that I had brought with me.

Over the next two days, I met various people who called at the house; we went to the main supermarket in town to stock up on all the necessary items to fill my cupboards; and in between everything, I drank endless cups of tea as I was quite dehydrated from the long flight as well as the heat. Gradually, I came to know all the practicalities necessary for safety, hygiene and electrical power.

Then it was time to go to the school and meet everybody there. This was the exciting moment for us all. I was taken into each class, where immediately the children stood up and sang a welcome song, waved tree branches, or chanted in a sing-song manner that I was most welcome. Both teachers and pupils had such beaming, beautiful faces. Many of the younger children wanted to hug me or at least touch my white arm as I passed. I certainly seemed to be a star attraction that day. I was in my element in this atmosphere of joy, energy and enthusiasm.

At lunchtime, I joined the Wellspring staff in the dining room where I ate my first meal of Ugandan food. I can't say it looked very appetising. It was a plateful of white food: matooke, which is mashed cooked banana; a creamy-looking groundnut sauce; white posho, which is ground maize; and a small Irish potato. I came to love all the

Ugandan food but the staff always teased me when it was matooke and groundnut sauce as they knew it was my least favourite meal of the week. I did soon acquire a taste for it, but beans would always remain my favourite choice.

I noticed that people were very quiet during the meal and gave their full attention to the plate of food in front of them. At the end of the meal though, when Mike introduced me as the new head teacher to the school, I was enveloped in a truly African welcome of loud cheering, clapping and waving. I felt at home with these people.

Over the coming days, I acclimatised to the heat. Fortunately, the area around Kampala is high above sea level and combined with the winds coming off Lake Victoria, a breeze is quite common. Back in England, friends were pulling out woollen jumpers and boots for the coming winter. Here all I needed every day was a sleeveless top with light trousers or a cotton skirt.

The house I rented had electricity supplying my washing machine, kettle, television, PC, light and hot water. On my third day, there was no electricity! Men cutting down a tree in the road had severed our line. That night I sat in the darkness with a spluttering candle. The night sounds seemed that much louder and more distinct now. I heard the continual high-pitched buzz of crickets, barking of dogs, passing traffic hooting regularly, music from a nearby bar… and then I heard footsteps passing my verandah window where I sat to keep cool.

I couldn't see anyone but a voice called out, 'Hello, Miss Holly.' Of course! It was our night watchman coming on duty. His small hut was near my verandah and in the dark it was comforting to hear the clack of his pans as he cooked his supper on a small stove, fed the guard dogs, patrolled the site for our security and responded if Mike called to him. This would occur regularly. I would hear a voice boom out through the dark: 'Steven!' No response. A few more, crosser and louder shouts of 'Steven!' Suddenly feet were heard scurrying across to the main house. I knew he had fallen asleep and would receive a reprimand.

Over the coming months, I tried to persuade him to stop washing his supper pots and pans at 5.00am. The clank and clink of these as he knocked them on the tap or dropped them on the ground woke me most mornings. A path to the dog kennels passed right under my bedroom window and his loud footsteps also woke me up often. Whenever I called to Steven to assist me with something, I could never see him in the darkness outside my door. I waited until he smiled and then I would see his beautiful white teeth gleaming in the night.

The first animal visitor in my house was a very large lizard in the hallway leading to my bedroom. I knew I would be stranded in the main room all night aware that it was moving around somewhere on the other side of the door. Steven came to my rescue and removed it so that I could sleep easily. It was a little more perturbing one morning when Joseph, our other night watchman, knocked on my bedroom window. I peered out sleepily to see him standing on the grass with an armed askari (security guard). It transpired that our alarm had been set off at their base and a van with half a dozen guards had arrived to confront a supposed incident. They kept checking by asking me, 'Are you sure you are all right?' I assured them that although I was on my own, as Mike and Beryl were away, I was completely fine and not being held hostage. They left feeling reassured and I made myself a cup of strong tea. At least I could rely on that alarm working if I ever needed it.

Whenever the electricity went off, it could be two days or longer before it returned. Wiring may have been stolen or a storm may have brought down a line but mainly it was 'power saving', with a chosen area foregoing their electricity for a set time, due to a limited supply provided nationally. I was so grateful my cooker was powered by gas. I could boil water in a saucepan and still make a cup of tea! It could be very annoying though when watching a TV programme at night and suddenly there would be instant silence and darkness, and you would have to flounder around to find a match and candle.

Towards the end of my first month, a public holiday was announced for the death of Obote, a Ugandan political leader who had lived in exile for many years. It seemed strange to me that such recognition was given to a man most people had deplored. However, a day free from work and routine duties was always welcomed and enjoyed by everyone. Over the years, I became accustomed to many public holidays celebrating significant national events as well as Christian and Muslim festivals.

Early Days

It became apparent during the first few staff meetings that my immediate priority was to build trust and relationship within the team. When I presented suggestions and ideas, I received no eye contact from anyone as their heads were bowed as if in prayer. If I asked a question, there was a reluctance for anyone to offer an answer. I explained that I needed to know their thoughts and ideas as I could easily offer ideas that may not be feasible and I needed their knowledge and experience. I wanted us to work as a team, with everybody's opinion and contribution being important. It seemed that this was a new way of management to them and one that would take some time to develop. I spent my first three months observing, reading and asking numerous questions.

I needed to be familiar with each area of the school's life and learning. I spent time becoming familiar with the Ugandan National Curriculum, the discipline methods, marking and assessment, and generally getting to know the children and staff. It soon became very clear that there had been a lack of leadership for a long time, resulting in most people doing what suited them best. Systems in place were being disregarded, rules were being broken, pupil discipline had become harsh and a sense of 'lethargy' had pervaded any steps towards improvement.

I discovered a cupboard containing piles of dusty storybooks that were in poor condition. Alongside them was a notebook where a record had been made of children who had borrowed a book for a small cost. The dates recorded there showed that no book had been taken for many months and there were only about ten pupils using the system. I took all the books outside into the sun where I discarded those that were too torn, cleaned the covers of the rest and sorted them into age categories. A local carpenter made and painted some sets of brightly coloured shelving for each class. Now every pupil could have easy and free access to good books in their classroom. This, to my mind, seemed a very positive step forward: I had a lot to learn!

In Uganda and most African countries, the school year runs from February to the end of November. The children returned from holiday excited to be back after nine weeks' holiday and to find a reading area full of colourful books in their classroom. I was horrified though during that first term as I saw how these books were handled. I would enter a classroom and find books on the floor, in dusty corners, book covers missing, pages torn or scribbled on, and teachers oblivious to this. I had imagined that the teachers would supervise the reading area and manage how the books were used. The system, or lack of system, was just not working.

There were many times like this when I had to return to my desk and think, 'What have I done wrong here?'

I recognised that I had initiated this scheme as, in my mind, a valuable learning tool was being wasted in a locked cupboard. However, I had not involved the staff in what I was doing and had just imposed the bookshelves on each classroom with enthusiasm and energy. Also, over time, I began to appreciate that books were a luxury item and far beyond a family or even school budget. I would need to train both teachers and pupils in handling and using the books and find a better way of utilising them. At this stage though, I collected them all up, explaining this would be a temporary measure only.

Later on, I reorganised all the books into a library area I had located and the classes visited weekly with their teachers. I spent time showing them wonderful picture storybooks, demonstrating how to turn each page, as previously I had watched pages just carelessly flicked over. When each child had selected a book, they were given a named, clear bag for storage purposes. This would keep it clean and undamaged back in the dusty classroom. Over the weeks, I watched their careless attitudes change as they began to enjoy and appreciate having a book in class, available at any time of the day. They now recognised the value of their book and wanted to take care of it.

Changing the mindset of the teachers was a lot harder. They were not used to a reading culture such as we enjoy in the West. In their minds, the most important thing was exam results. They could not see how a storybook could assist as it was totally unrelated to the specific curriculum matter. In addition, they felt there was no spare time within the curriculum demands to allow free reading. Their own education had been based entirely around textbooks and I was not sure they appreciated the library system as much as their pupils. Sadly, when sets of lovely storybooks are donated to a school, they can remain on a shelf in the head teacher's office. Work has to be done in conjunction with the staff to ensure the resources donated are used fully.

Most British schools hold a 'book week' or 'book day' and I wanted to hold a similar event for our children. The teachers were aghast at the thought of suspending the usual timetable and were concerned about losing time to cover the term's curriculum. I explained we could still teach maths, science and English but through stories and project work. They took a lot of convincing but at least I was happy that now they were confident to air their thoughts and concerns. I gave several workshops to illustrate how a particular book could be used as a stimulus for art, drama, music, as well as core subjects. We allowed enough time for groups of teachers to work together in preparing for this week. I was very encouraged to see their own original ideas being shared and discussed.

On our last day of the week, we held a hat competition where nearly every child had made an effort at home to wear some kind of head attire. We had straw boaters decorated with fresh flowers, paper bags folded into peaked caps, a hessian sack wrapped like a turban as well as some more traditional stylish hats. I had a collection of hats for children who were unable to provide one and all the teachers entered into the spirit of the event and wore a hat too.

We opened the school to the parents that afternoon and gave an exhibition to show all the work that had been produced during the week. They were astonished to see amazing artwork, pictorial graphs, poetry, scientific experiments as well as a book for each class that depicted their story. These class books were placed in the library to be enjoyed by everyone in future.

I breathed a sigh of relief that it had all been so successful and enjoyable. When I heard teachers chatting and saying it must be repeated the next year, I felt very grateful to them. They had overcome their fears of the unknown and stepped out into a freer and more creative way of teaching that was completely new to them.

We all enjoyed cakes and sodas together at the end of the final day. We were starting to work like a team and my heart was singing.

All Change

In my first term at Wellspring, I had wondered why the children wore PE uniform on two days of the week, as I had never seen a PE lesson actually take place. It was explained to me that this system enabled the official school uniform to be washed and dried on those days. I decided to search and see if we had any equipment hidden away for PE. I found a few items and bought some more before setting up a timetable for all the classes to have at least one lesson outside.

I led a workshop to demonstrate simple team games and activities although I was well aware that the teachers considered such lessons a waste of their teaching time, as there was no exam in PE. I did try to suggest that fresh air, fun and exercise would stimulate the children's brains and they would be more alert for the following lesson. It was some time before I could relax and be assured that the lessons were continuing. Until then I had to monitor and insist on this extra subject being included in the curriculum.

Knowing the teachers to be reluctant with PE lessons, I was most surprised, when planning our sports day, that they suggested we include throwing the javelin and the discus! Nobody had any training for this, so the idea was quickly squashed by my health and safety concerns. However, the activities we did agree on gained Olympic status in the training programme. Each class walked regularly to the upper field above our school where I could see them from the playground and wondered just how long they would continue in such heat and dust.

Enthusiasm was high and a competitive spirit evolved. Team banners were painted, hats were made for the nursery pupils, songs were composed and generally the excitement was escalating. We used our school buses to transport them on the day to a nearby swimming pool and play area. No fear of rain stopping play. The sun was shining brightly, the pool was sparkling and the chicken was being prepared for lunch. Parents sat in a shaded area and cheered on the competitors. A national television crew was filming and interviewing some pupils. One older boy renowned for his outgoing personality explained how proud he had felt at winning his swimming race. They didn't know he had not been in the swimming races and innocently congratulated him on his achievement. I just smiled to myself at the ingenuity and opportunism he displayed always. He had the potential to be in either Parliament or the criminal world: we were working hard to influence him along a positive path!

Later in the day, a sudden, massive crash shocked everyone when a large loudspeaker fell sideways. Fortunately, nobody was near it just at that moment. At the end of the day, when I thanked all the parents for their enthusiasm and support, I mentioned this near disaster. I reminded them that Wellspring was a Christian school where we prayed for our pupils and their families. We had seen God's hand of protection covering us and we were thankful for the safety of our pupils and their parents.

As well as sport events, we gave musical presentations to parents on our open days. In England, I had always held responsibility for music within schools, so I had plenty of resources and ideas. I threw all my energy and effort into rehearsals as I wanted a good standard to be reached in the performance. It was disconcerting, though, to find myself busy, hot and sweaty organising children while teachers sat at the side watching me or even chatting on their mobile phones! They seemed to think that if I was prepared to take a lead, they were free just to observe and rest.

It was finally explained to me that I needed to respect my role as the head teacher of the school. For the performance, I was there to represent the prestige and authority of my position by sitting in the front row in a stately manner. I was the mzungu[4] head teacher, not a cheerleader. So that is what I did. I handed over full responsibility to the teachers and their efforts did not disappoint me.

I have wonderful memories of Christmas plays where Mary and Joseph were pulled across the stage sitting on a wooden zebra, our Indian pupils performed magnificent dances in glorious outfits and classes enacted cultural and traditional dancing in grass skirts and face paint. I provided a set of claves when a nursery class were learning the song, *Knock, Knock, Knock at the door*[5]. I asked my carpenter to cut me some rounded wooden sticks. When these were returned to the stock cupboard after the performance, I was amused to see that a

---

[4] A white person
[5] *Knock! Knock!* by Mark and Helen Johnson; Out of the Ark Music

teacher had labelled them 'knocking sticks'. This was the same cupboard from where I ran out screaming one day: two live chickens were in there but I was told they were for teacher Mabel's tea that evening. Without fridges, meat must be bought fresh and eaten that day.

We were learning to laugh together by now and work together as friends as well as colleagues. We had come a long way from the early days of bowed heads and non-participation.

A B C

There is huge pressure on all schools throughout Africa to perform well in examinations. Education is the doorway into a better future and every family wants their children to be successful. Therefore, all teaching and learning is focused on the exams. Each term, every class sits three tests: at the start, middle and end. These papers are then collated and parents receive them at the end of term. This is the method used to reinforce learning and monitor what has been understood. Even the three-year-olds in the first class will sit with a teacher and complete their test papers. When they enter the primary section, they are examined on each year's curriculum, culminating in their final exam in year P7, known as PLE (Primary Leaving Examinations), where they are questioned on all the work of the past seven years.

Wellspring School began as a nursery school in 2000 with just eight pupils aged three or four. When I joined the school in 2005, these pupils had reached P3 so we did not face these important exams until 2009. The whole community was anxious to see how this group of pupils would perform. There was doubt that we could achieve top results as they considered our school day to be too short. We began lessons at 8.00am and the older pupils finished at 5.00pm. It is expected that most children from around the age of eight will attend boarding schools, as there they can study until 9.00pm as well as during the weekend. It also means they are free from home domestic duties and distractions of younger children. Sadly, many children begin in Wellspring Nursery but leave after three or four years to enter a boarding school.

All fears were allayed, however, as our 2009 first exam results were excellent and we continued to improve with even higher results year on year. We were encouraged to see that this influenced the parents to keep their children at Wellspring right through to P7. We had treated them as individuals with a right to have time to relax, play and be a child. We had not anxiously crammed their brains to overcapacity, but we had set high expectations for every individual pupil to achieve their best. Our pupils were cheerful, confident and articulate, assured enough to participate in debates and discussions, learning to express their own opinions and ideas.

Parents often commented positively on the difference in attitude and demeanour between Wellspring pupils and those from other local schools. I particularly remember the son of one of our teachers who was struggling academically and was very unhappy at a school in the locality. He was being beaten by teachers, due to his poor performance and attitude. He came to Wellspring and we saw a fearful, timid and apprehensive young boy who walked about school with his head down and his body stooped. After just a few weeks, I saw a different person altogether: he was smiling, laughing with his friends, making eye contact with adults and moving around school with a new energy and motivation.

We held a policy that banned hitting, slapping, pinching or any form of physical chastisement. This is not usual practice in Ugandan schools and some parents doubted our methods. The matter was raised at one public parents' meeting as they wanted to know our reason for not disciplining our pupils. I had to correct them and say, 'Of course we discipline children, but we have found and use a far more effective and humane way than beating them.'

New teachers took a while to adjust to our methods and needed to be monitored as well as trained since they were not familiar with any system other than beating. Each year I led a staff workshop on discipline, in which we could be open about the matter and come to positive conclusions. However, I found it necessary eventually to have a signed agreement from each new recruit that they understood our policy and that not abiding by it would result in dismissal. In time, two teachers did have to be dismissed over this very issue.

I was not afraid to confront important issues and the staff became more secure in knowing their boundaries whilst being constantly respected, encouraged and praised publicly. When I did have to deal with an area that needed improvement, the teachers often thanked me for helping them to achieve higher standards. The pupils in their class were regarded as 'son' or 'daughter' and they wanted the best for them.

In my first year, I noticed that each school had a motto and we did not have one. I looked at several mottoes that were being used. These ranged from 'Aim High', 'Be a God-Fearing Citizen', 'Hard Work Pays' to 'Educating for Tomorrow'. I wanted our motto to embrace our hopes for each individual and our hard work to achieve their potential. I was aware of the ABC motif used in the campaign to halt the spread of AIDS[6] and also noticed that our school's letter-headed paper included a picture of a chalkboard showing 'ABC'. I took those same three letters and conceived the following:

Achieving the Best for each Child, often represented visually as:

A chieving the

B est for each

C hild

That motto would underpin all our efforts and help ensure we gave equal support and attention to each pupil to achieve their individual best.

---

[6] The ABC motif in the AIDS campaign is known widely across Africa; it stands for: Abstain, Be faithful, Condomise.

Name, Please

The school year running from February to the end of November means the months of January and February are very busy times for the staff in the school office. By January, my assistant Irene and I had everything purchased and organised for the incoming pupils which included sixty or more three-year-old entrants to our nursery.

When school officially opened, parents and pupils arrived early and created a queue around our office, along the corridor and out into the car park, where we set out a seating area. In my first year, we took our school fees in cash. This required counting, recording and receipting by hand. Very few parents gave the full term's fees in one payment, so a running balance needed to be recorded throughout the term with reminder letters sent to parents about their outstanding balance.

I needed to be fully alert and attuned to the Ugandan money notes as I counted, recorded and kept note of the remaining balance to be paid. At the same time, all new pupils were buying their school and PE uniforms. The set consisted of school shirt, shorts or skirt, socks, scarf, PE shorts and T-shirt, all of which needed to be tried on for size. With the different permutations of clothing required, calculating each parent's bill was complicated. At the same time, a three-year-old child could be sobbing at the prospect of now being left by their parents.

I have never worked under such pressure and at such a fast pace as in these first few days of the term. Parents were anxious to complete their transactions and get to work, some pupils were inconsolable as we took them into the nursery hall and we were frantically trying to sell, record, add, subtract, and count in a vigilant way a huge amount of cash. Fortunately, not all pupils return to school the first week of term as many delay their return from the village where they have spent their long holiday with relatives. This means, however, that you have no idea of your number on roll until at least three weeks into the first term. It was a huge relief when we introduced a new system whereby parents paid school fees into the bank and presented us with a bank slip only.

One of my first difficulties for recording payments and writing receipts by hand had been how to spell names correctly. Moses Akimbo

Katamba – 'Would that need one t or two?' All the names were completely new to me and it took a while to become familiar with them and connect names to specific pupils. We were often delighted by new Indian families arriving to register their children with our school. We had a friend in Mr Patel, a local businessman, who encouraged all new Indian migrants to register immediately with us. These pupils were very welcome and contributed much to our school through their polite, gentle manners and their unique culture demonstrated through dress, dance and festivals. One tiny new Indian boy in the nursery really struggled to be separated from his mother. He refused to remove his rucksack from his back and we discovered that if we let him sit at his table with it, he settled more happily. This continued for about six weeks until he was finally willing to hang it on his peg. This was a significant milestone for him and our willingness to be flexible allowed him to establish security in his own particular way.

I took great delight in our nursery children, who gave me an enthusiastic welcome every time I entered their classroom. Many of them had little experience of leaving their homes, remaining in an enclosed environment with a maid each day whilst parents were busy working. They soon adjusted to the demands of a busy school day, but very often by lunchtime, a few had their heads on their tables and were fast asleep, ready to be collected and taken home.

School Days

One early morning as I arrived at school, I found several children congregated at the main entrance and not inside their classrooms. Many parents dropped their children at 7.00am, as they needed to drive to work in town. Each younger class had a box of toys they played with then. That day, teachers in the nursery hall had heard a sudden shout from a small group playing but thought they were teasing each other with the plastic lizard that most of them disliked. Further shouts alerted them to the fact that there was a black mamba in the Lego box! Our maintenance man was fetched and as he proceeded to kill it, I took photos from my safe position standing on top of a desk. This was my first sighting of a black mamba but I was aware it is one of Africa's deadliest snakes and its bite will cause death within seconds. Ugandans fear it greatly.

A month later it was my birthday and I organised some snacks and sodas for the staff. There was a lot of suspicious giggling and amusement when they presented me with a small package to open. This alerted me to open it with caution. As I peeled back the paper gingerly, a wiggly leg wobbled in my face and I screamed and threw it across the floor in a nervous reaction. It was only the dreaded plastic lizard wrapped to entertain and wish me a happy birthday. They all knew my sense of humour and that I would enjoy their joke.

The following year, I bought the birthday sodas again and we met in a classroom. They had cooked a plate of sausages for everyone as a snack but provided me with a special individual delicacy. It was two cow's feet cooked and sitting in gravy in a blue plastic bowl. I had never experienced this before so it really was a birthday surprise and apparently a sign of honour.

Our staff meetings could be challenging at times, but I did not expect the issue of circumcision to appear on the agenda. On one occasion, I was explaining some practical matters to everyone, when I was interrupted suddenly by a loud commotion at the doorway. A group of people holding weapons and shields whilst wearing grass skirts, masks and what looked like war-paint on their faces burst upon the scene. My heart began to thump anxiously, responding to the adrenalin-fuelled beat of the drumming that invaded our quiet meeting. My staff jumped up gleefully and joined in the dancing and excitement that followed. I was utterly bemused by now, until one kind teacher stopped to explain to me what was happening. Every two years, one of the largest ethnic groups in Uganda, the Basoga, prepare for the circumcision of their young men. This involves a large, elaborate ceremony and celebration for which they seek funding to cover the costs. Their loud rejoicing was intended to encourage our support and generosity. I wasn't feeling too generous just at that moment; more alarmed and out of my comfort zone. The excitable group moved to the shops outside Wellspring but we could hear the drums and singing still. I tried to restore order and dignity for our meeting to resume but we had lost impetus and after a short while I brought it to a close and postponed matters for another time.

School trips are of course a highlight of any school year. In my work in England, I had organised and led many day and residential trips. I was rather amazed though when the staff suggested organising a trip that would take the whole school out for a day. I tried to discuss the practical problems this would raise but they considered my doubts and fears unfounded. I felt that as I had no experience of a trip in this country, I should heed their confident and enthusiastic plans. Five coaches were booked to take everyone to the zoo in Entebbe and then across to the airport site. The children began arriving at school really early in their excitement for the day ahead. The coaches arrived an hour late and then there was a further delay because the chapatis were still being cooked for lunch by the school kitchen. Everyone remained very cheerful and patient and not at all stressed by the delays. Eventually the children boarded the coaches, crates of soda were allocated to each coach and I waved them all off-site as they cheered and waved excitedly. Unfortunately, I was obliged to remain behind to attend some important staffing interviews.

That evening, parents began to arrive at the time we were expecting the coaches to return. Traffic jams in Kampala are notorious for causing long delays and our coaches were caught up in such a scenario. Parents remained cheerful and patient but I began to fret and worry. Finally, we saw the first coach weaving its way slowly down Wellspring Road. The older children looked happy and satisfied as they disembarked. The young nursery children looked utterly exhausted.

They had to be physically helped down the steps and steered towards their classrooms as most of them seemed disorientated and dazed. It had been just too much for them. From then on, I insisted that only one year group at a time went on a trip so that the length of day and the content of the sites visited could be age-related.

One of our favourite trips was when we took the top class to Jinja, an important attraction for nationals and tourists alike. The River Nile flows through there and farther downstream the specific spot that marks the source of the Nile can be seen. Many other sites can be visited: there is a memorial statue to Ghandi, a power-generating dam and, at that point in time, the Bugagali Falls[7].

A group of children from my home church had fundraised to cover the cost of this special trip. They knew the top class was approaching the last year at the school and that none of them had visited Jinja before, even though it was only 70 kilometres away. The class teachers were just as excited as the children, as they had not been to the site either. We had the most wonderful day together. At the Falls, a tourist attraction involves a small payment to watch young men soar down the Falls hanging onto nothing but a yellow jerry can. This is extremely risky and some people have lost their lives as a result. It is a money-making venture, however, so people are prepared to take such risks. Despite the clamour of the children for me to pay to watch this demonstration, I didn't wish to encourage this risky behaviour that might become a career choice for some of my pupils later. They were so happy when some willing tourists made a payment and we all watched the daring feat. It was hugely exhilarating to watch, and fortunately, both young men returned completely unhurt.

We moved farther up the bank to an area where we could sit and have lunch. We had booked to have chicken and chips provided here for everyone. Having distributed sodas and ensured everyone had their lunch, I sat to enjoy mine. I had just taken a bite of my delicious roasted chicken when something brushed past my head. I thought somebody had thrown a jumper or something across, but then I looked down and realized I had no chicken now in my left hand. A large fish eagle was spotted flying up into a tree with my piece of juicy chicken. I couldn't believe that out of our group it had picked on me to victimise and steal away my lunch. Although everyone offered sympathy, it was also very

---

[7] These were later flooded to create a second dam.

amusing. When reports were written up the next day, each child had to write about one of their highlights. The stolen chicken got the highest rating, even more than the jumping daredevils. It was sharing such moments as these that joined our hearts together in fun, love and friendship. Those children will always remember that day and the joy and laughter we shared together. I certainly treasure the memory.

Fire can be a very frightening and dangerous experience. When I was working in a Surrey school, a serious fire took place. It began in a cloakroom where a troubled child lit a cigarette lighter before returning to class. Fire broke out and the school building was evacuated. One class needed to jump from a window and another class had to crawl along the corridor below the rising smoke. Fortunately, nobody was injured, but fears and anxieties remained in many for a while after. As a head teacher in three schools, it was my responsibility to ensure a fire evacuation procedure was practised each term and recorded officially. Having seen the trauma of a school fire, I was very diligent about this duty and although I portrayed a professional confidence and calm, memories easily stirred up past emotions.

My school in Uganda had no arrangements for emergency evacuations and I soon introduced a fire drill each term. I had been reading, with horror, newspaper accounts where school fires had taken the lives of many young students. The use of candles and cooking stoves added to the possibility of a fire and the fact that all windows are secured with metal grids to guard against robbery meant windows could not be used as an escape route.

My great friends and directors of Wellspring lost their beloved niece in a very bad fire in a top school in Kampala. They supported me fully in introducing fire safety precautions into the school.

Tragically, our own school community did lose a young nursery pupil in a home fire. Esther had been sleeping when the fire began and her father tried to enter the building to rescue her and had to be held back by neighbours who were anxious to save his own life. Everything in their house was lost. To lose a daughter this way is unimaginable pain. We stood with the community and family as they buried such a small coffin and watched the family face this devastating tragedy.

Back at school, it was my role to lead our school community in a special remembrance assembly. I talked about Esther and showed pictures that she had drawn in her exercise books that term. They were simple pencil drawings by a carefree child who was happy and safe in her school life. I described the fun she had shared with her class friends and how her last day with them had been a cheerful and enjoyable time and that was how we could remember her in future. I explained that loving is sometimes painful. Usually we were celebrating success, achievement or special events together but now we were a family sharing loss and great sadness. At the end, I suggested we stayed sitting to sing one of our favourite songs, so we could reflect on the words and feel strengthened by each other. As we began to sing, 'We are family, we are one,' a few of the younger children at the front placed their arms around the shoulders of the child either side of them. This was copied spontaneously by the other classes behind. It was like a ripple of love expressed right through the hall as both pupils and staff linked in this way and swayed in harmony as they sang the song. It was a very poignant and moving moment in the life of our school.

Afterwards, the children led quietly out of the hall to begin their break-time. It was then that we discovered several pupils who were distressed and very upset. Losing Esther had brought back memories of relatives they had lost in similar fires and all their emotions were surfacing and being expressed. Very quickly, we set up a quiet classroom where at least a dozen children of all ages came to us and had the opportunity to talk, remember, cry, ask questions and receive love from us as they processed their own thoughts and feelings. Several asked us to pray with them which we did willingly and they returned to class later feeling more settled and peaceful.

We are family we are one, we are family we are one.
We are children of our father,
We are family, we are one.

Charles Groot

Changed Lives

Our pupils loved being at school. They enjoyed learning and being together with friends and teachers. Their standard of behaviour was excellent and they participated with enthusiasm and energy. The style of learning is very different to that in UK schools though and the desks are generally in rows, facing the chalkboard. Each teacher introduces the lesson content, writes notes on the board and the important facts are recorded by the children in order to memorise them for exams. There is little practical work or group work. It is a disciplined, formal approach which allows little room for self-expression, opinion, problem-solving or the use of creative imagination. In fact, when these less formal methods of learning are introduced, the behaviour appears to worsen. Really, this is because they are not used to such freedom and flexibility and do not possess the self-discipline necessary. I began to notice that although behaviour was so good in class, many classes left their rooms for break-time in a very disorderly and unruly manner.

I began by working with the very top class which then was P4 and had seven pupils only. As they left their room, fighting, kicking and chasing would immediately break out and quite aggressive behaviour was demonstrated. Their room was the closest to my office so I would ensure that I was in that area before the lesson ended. On many occasions, they had to return to class, sit down at their desks, hear how I expected them as the eldest class to lead out and then go out in a suitable way. At the same time, I was always looking for opportunities to praise them individually or collectively and build up their own motivation.

I realized that they were not doing any of the creative areas of the curriculum, such as art. This neglect of certain parts of the National Curriculum was one I knew I had to address across the whole school. As a start, I initiated a series of art lessons myself with this particular class. One material we decided to use was clay so the class teacher and I took them outside under the tree for shade and we allowed them to create their own piece of pottery. One boy lacked total confidence in himself and was very isolated from the others who seemed either to tease him or ignore him. He always sat on his own at the back of the class, never ventured to answer questions, cried very easily and was generally performing very poorly in his work. This pottery art work was a turning point for Nicholas. He had designed and created a bird. The others all gathered round him at the end of the lesson and began to praise and congratulate him. It was far better than any of their attempts. As the series of lessons continued that term, his natural ability in art was obvious. The recognition and kudos this brought him changed his whole outlook and it opened up a new way forward for Nicholas. He found a new confidence, began to interact in lessons and gradually over time his academic performance improved. Three years later, he achieved a high second division in the final exams where previously he had been expected to fail or attain just a division four. When this lad left us to go to secondary school, we knew we had given him a good foundation and that he could aspire and work for greater achievement. He often returned to visit and we heard how well he was doing. It was a thrilling experience to participate in changing futures for children.

I was pleased with all of them in this class. Having deliberately focused on them to give input, discipline, encouragement and love, they responded very quickly. They began to mature, take more responsibility for their behaviour and attitudes, and became more cohesive as a group. I became so fond of them and they secured a very special place in my heart. When they left, it was a wrench to say goodbye, but I felt we had done our best to prepare them for the challenges they would face ahead. As our first cohort to reach P7, they achieved exceptionally well in their exams. I was equally as proud of their results as I was of the people they had become. It had been well worth the commitment of time, effort and love.

Close to our school lived a more professional family than the other families in this particular class. They paid fees and expected their son to perform well and move to a top boarding school after Wellspring. He had frequent days of absence though, due to a stomach complaint. His parents had taken him for several tests but nothing had been discovered and no improvement was forthcoming. He continually complained of stomach pains, headaches and discomfort and generally displayed a very lethargic approach to lessons of any kind. At times, I would allow him to sit in a comfortable chair in my office and relax there for a while before returning to class again.

One particular morning, he appeared despondent about the situation. I couldn't see how it was going to improve and his work was suffering as a result. I suggested we pray there and then about his health. In a school in England this would be deemed unsuitable, but in Uganda, where the majority of families attended church, it was an acceptable practice. I also felt that as I had authority as head of the school, I was in a unique position to use that authority spiritually. I prayed with him and very soon he returned to class.

The next morning, I was in the playground at break when I suddenly spotted Brian. He was running energetically around the playground, arms up in the air, whooping as he ran. This was not usual. He normally sat still, looking very glum and unhappy while his friends chased each other around. When I called him over, he explained that all his pain, discomfort and fatigue had completely left him. He seemed invigorated.

This state of well-being continued but the sickness had become an excuse for opting out of any active participation and this took longer to change. I needed to gently but firmly put some pressure on him to apply his good brain fully to his studies now. He eventually adjusted to a healthier approach to work, physical exercise and homework. The physical and the academic had become interwoven in the problem but that negative thread had now been broken. He continued to remain well and obtained a high grade at the end. When he left, his parents expressed their gratitude for a school that had handled their son with respect, understanding, care and encouragement. These were the values our pupils deserved and they blossomed with such nurturing.

Barbara, in a class below, also had health problems but hers were of a very serious and debilitating nature. Illness had taken the life of her mother, and her father worked away from home, so she was cared for by her single grandmother. Barbara often missed school when she was sick or when she was attending regular hospital appointments. Obviously, her illness itself and her poor attendance record impacted on her school progress. By nature, she was a shy, reserved child with a very gentle and reticent manner. Her close friends, however, were the opposite. They embraced all of school life with an enthusiasm and cheerful humour that was infectious. They never neglected her, and included her in all their energetic activities and ideas. They were always kind, generous, thoughtful and good friends to her as well as to each other.

One weekend, Barbara's grandmother suddenly became ill. She very quickly deteriorated and died. Our community was shocked and saddened by this loss and we were very concerned for Barbara. At the burial, it was profoundly moving when our shy, timid schoolgirl knelt by the side of her grandmother's coffin and verbalised publicly her gratitude and appreciation for all the love and care she had received from her. She had lost so much but she was able still to express thanks and gratitude.

We followed the family to the area prepared for the actual burial. Whenever Grandmother Lydia had visited me in my school office, she would follow the tradition of kneeling in respect to me. I always took her hand and lifted her up again but she was of the culture that still used this way of greeting respectfully. Although we did not share the same language, I knew how much she appreciated the care we gave her granddaughter. That afternoon, I did not kneel physically, but in my heart I did kneel before Lydia. She was a woman I had grown to love and respect. I had recently returned from Israel where I had bought a small wooden cross made of olive wood. I had taken it with me and I dropped it in silently with Lydia. My prayer was that the love Barbara had now lost would be taken up by her community and she would receive the help and care she so needed.

Africa: Birthright and Calling

PART THREE

Cultural Crossroads

Stand at the crossroads and look; ask for the ancient paths, ask where the good way is, and walk in it, and you will find rest for your souls.

Jeremiah 6:16

The ride home.

Survival Mode

A familiar advert for a cooking oil named Fortune is displayed on large billboards around Uganda. It declares that, 'Everyone deserves a fortune.'

The majority of Ugandan people struggle to provide the basic necessities of salt, sugar, flour and oil. A fortune in financial terms is an unrealistic dream, or maybe an aspiration for some. Most families are struggling each day for survival with regards to the provision of food, clothing and adequate shelter. Education is an additional financial burden that produces the most anxiety when economic pressures limit schooling. Many families live within a small unit the size of a British beach hut. They have no running water or electricity, and heavy rain causes extreme flooding, which brings subsequent distress and discomfort. Daily tasks are undertaken outside when the weather permits. Clothes are washed by hand and draped across bushes to dry; food is prepared, cooked and eaten; and social activities such as hair-braiding, games of Ludo and general gossip are shared together outside in the open.

Children will happily spend hours amusing themselves by creating make-believe homes using earth, stones, sticks and leaves. In every family unit, the older children willingly take care of their younger siblings as well as helping with all domestic duties. Most of the children I knew would not receive birthday or Christmas presents but would probably receive a new outfit to wear for Christmas itself. During one of my training courses for head teachers, a member returned from the lunch break looking very happy. He laid out on the table three differently coloured, small racing cars, one for each of his children. His subsequent comment really brought home to me the difference in expectations and attitudes of families in Africa. He said, 'My three children will be so grateful for these gifts at Christmas.' What a contrast from the exceedingly high expectations and attitudes displayed by our youngsters in the West. Such gratefulness was always exhibited by my Ugandan friends whenever they received a little extra or a surprise gift.

Also, when they had a little more, it was often generously shared so that others could benefit too.

To sit with friends in their home on a raffia mat and be served black tea and possibly a bread roll for refreshment was a privilege I valued so much. Their welcoming hospitality enhances the simplest of gatherings and you are left feeling united by love in the most unique way. Such friendship is priceless and sharing times together is always an honour. Now that I am living back in England, I can no longer pass on all my empty glass coffee jars, plastic-lidded food containers, past newspapers or used gift wrapping. It was so satisfying to give such items to my friends and colleagues whom I knew would use them to good purpose. Daily basic provisions are purchased loose and placed in small plastic or paper bags, so a set of three large coffee jars became an effective storage set for sugar, flour or salt.

Where small rats enter food cupboards, it is very beneficial to have properly secured and lidded containers. On one occasion, I had bought some special chocolate and decorations for a time when a couple I knew were going to use my house for their honeymoon. I placed them all in a wardrobe until the wedding month neared. Not long after, I discovered the biggest rat I had ever seen running from that bedroom. I traced its path back to the wardrobe and found the bag with half-eaten and chewed chocolate bars. Disposing of what was left, I realized chocolate was a good enticement for future rat-catching!

I knew I was regarded with some perplexity in Uganda. It is most unusual there for a woman to remain unmarried and never bear children. 'Family' acts as a foundation stone in a society that provides little or no provision for healthcare, pensions, care of the elderly, or assistance when faced with unexpected accidents or disasters. It is expected that all females will marry and produce children. In fact, if a woman fails to produce children, she will often be discarded by her husband, who will find another wife in the hope that this one will be able to produce offspring. As a single woman, who had never borne children, I was regarded by many as a complete enigma. Added to this was the fact that I lived happily on my own in a very large house and was not perturbed by this in any way. When darkness arrives, most people want the security and comfort of company with whom they can share their meals, conversation and evening. I was frequently asked by both children and adults, 'Are you not afraid living in a big house all on your own?'

On one occasion, I did receive a marriage proposal. Through attending area meetings for head teachers, I came to know some local heads and offered them lifts in my vehicle for future times. At a later stage, I was approached by Thomas, who declared his love and desire to marry me. Having explained that our age gap was not conducive to a relationship, we were able to work together professionally still. When he later asked if I would refer him to other European women, I was not so impressed.

Having various crazy experiences throughout my time in Uganda, I concluded that you needed to be slightly mad to survive and I was encouraged by the words of Lewis Carroll in *Alice in Wonderland:*

> *'You're entirely bonkers!! But I'll tell you a secret, all the best people are.'* [8]

---

[8] *Alice's Adventures in Wonderland;* Lewis Carroll (1865)

Glorious Food

Food plays an important role in all cultures and acts as an expression of welcome and hospitality. Ugandan people will always want to bless a visitor by providing a drink and something to eat, even at a sacrificial cost to themselves. It is usual for a family to eat two cooked meals a day where they are able to afford this. Our Western style of a light sandwich lunch would be most unacceptable and salad would never satisfy a hungry Ugandan person. All Wellspring staff ate a cooked lunch that was provided for them each day but they always cooked again when they returned home in the evening. Such meals take a lot of work; from the shopping for fresh food and preparation of this to the cooking over a charcoal stove, all after having arrived home at maybe 9.00pm.

No food is ever eaten without handwashing before the meal or snack. At a large function, a bowl of water and towel will be brought to each person to enable hands to be washed prior to the meal. Cooked food is kept covered always with lids or cloths. I once made the mistake of passing a doughnut to my office colleague by hand. She pointed out to me that I needed to put it on a plate and cover the doughnut with a saucer before handing it across to her. In an environment full of dust, flies and insects, such practice is purely sensible and hygienic. I remember when youth teams visited Wellspring, staff were surprised that they often moved around the dining room while eating fruit or chapati. Children are taught from a young age to remain sitting while eating any food. In my busy-ness in my work, I often walked about the school compound with a mug of tea in my hand, but my teachers came to understand how much I enjoyed my tea and accepted my habit.

For a time, I was a member of a small ladies' group that met in the home of its leader. I learnt a lesson in etiquette regarding the peeling and eating of a banana. I was given a small banana for a snack and I peeled the complete skin, placed it on the coffee table and began to eat the banana. 'No, no, Miss Holly! Not like that.' I was shown that I needed to just peel back the skin gradually as I ate the banana, so that my hand never touched the actual fruit going into my mouth. It made obvious sense really and I learnt my lesson.

Within this same group, we decided we wanted to cook a meal one evening for our church leaders. We planned the menu and then items of food were allocated to each person. During our cost calculations, it was an eye-opener to realize that salt, sugar and oil required costings. Provision of this meal would be an expensive sacrifice but it was still undertaken with cheerful enthusiasm. I have observed that even young children are willing to share a treat whereby a biscuit is broken in two to be handed to another child nearby. This attitude could be very humbling at times.

I saw that in times of economic hardship, many families were forced to limit themselves to one cooked meal a day. The usual meal would be beans with posho (cooked maize) or matooke (cooked bananas). Pupils attending boarding school tend to eat this every day for lunch. At our school, the children received a drink and snack at each morning break-time. Most pupils leave home very early to walk or travel to school, allowing no time for breakfast so the snack is very much welcomed. A cooked lunch is also provided and this maintains their energy levels for work in the afternoon.

It was traditional at Wellspring for all staff to receive a Christmas gift. This was often in the form of food provisions such as sugar, oil or flour or even, on occasion, a live chicken. One year we all bought a small present for a person whose name we had selected from a hat. It was wonderful to see the delight on people's faces as they received a set of glasses, mugs or saucepans while others had a plastic wash bowl, a piece of fabric or some placemats.

During the holiday, they would travel back to their family village and share the celebrations with a special meal on Christmas Day. The festivities were short though and did not extend longer, due to financial restraints. I always enjoyed inviting people into my home for a Christmas dinner when I was staying in Uganda over the holiday. I usually wrapped up a very small gift for each person. Over the years, a friend, Moses, came several times and was delighted to receive a gift, as it was the first he had ever received on Christmas Day in his whole life. Such moments are unique and helped to make my own Christmas special and rewarding.

Every other year, I travelled to England for the Christmas holiday. After enjoying many food treats and good meals there, I usually put on weight. This would always be commented on by friends and colleagues when I returned to Uganda. 'Oh, look at your fat arms now.' 'Miss Holly, you have added much weight from being in England.' It took me many conversations to convince people that I was not feeling complimented by their comments. I did not want to gain weight, but they regarded it as a positive sign that I had enjoyed many good meals. In their mindset, it merited a favourable comment.

This attitude helped explain the method pupils used to distinguish between two teachers with the same name. One they called 'teacher Patricia', the other 'fat teacher Patricia'! They couldn't understand why I wanted them to stop this identification method. One of the classes had been studying comparisons in their English lessons. In their assembly presentation to the school, they illustrated a comparison by three different-sized pupils holding up three words: 'fat', 'fatter' and 'fattest'. The boy holding the card with 'fattest' on it was an immensely overweight child. He held up his word proudly. Everyone laughed at his cheerful humour and showed no concern with this illustration.

Mind Your Language

Although English was the common language, it was interesting to hear how words and phrases were used differently from the way we would use them. A child aged four would be described as, 'He's making four.' A hurt finger would be, 'My finger is paining me.' I still find myself using some of the Ugandan ways in conversation. A word used often is 'sorry'. If I stubbed my toes on a desk, or dropped a file suddenly, my work colleagues would say, 'Oh, sorry.' This was their way of showing sympathy and attention for a mishap or misfortune.

There had been a long weekend due to a public holiday for a Muslim festival. Returning to work, I phoned my car mechanic to arrange a service for that week. When I had ended my conversation with John, my office bursar spoke to me really crossly. 'Miss Holly, how could you speak like that to John?' I was confused and explained that I had arranged a car service and sympathised with him because he had been unwell throughout the short holiday. 'No, you didn't,' she replied, 'you told him it was a shame he was unwell. What is shameful about being unwell? Poor John.' There was no point in desperately trying to explain how we use the word 'shame' in more than one context. It had been interpreted as shame such as disgrace or being dishonourable. From that point on, I self-corrected whenever I nearly said, 'Oh, what a shame,' and said instead, 'Oh, I am sorry.'

A response to which it took me time to adjust was how people reacted to illness. I went into the office one day with a very bad cold, headache and high temperature. When I explained to Joy how I was feeling, I anticipated some sympathetic words but instead she replied, 'Oh, you will be fine, Holly, just fine; don't you worry at all.' I did not feel fine and that wasn't really what I wanted to hear just then. I came to understand and recognise that some people used positive encouragement and even denial of problems to foster faith for improvement. Even when you meet someone and ask how they are, they may reply positively with, 'I'm fine,' even though they could be experiencing really difficult circumstances or even bereavement.

Africans always take time to converse fully when they meet you; there is no hurried acknowledgement without a pause for communication. Time is given to ask about the welfare of the family members, how you spent the weekend or even, how is the home? Whenever we greeted each other in the mornings at work, time was given for a proper greeting to each other. One morning, I was in a hurry to get exam papers distributed to all the classrooms. I passed teacher Stella and let her know I had put her papers on her desk earlier. She looked at me and quietly said, 'Good morning, Miss Holly, how was your weekend?' I was ashamed of myself, and apologised immediately and gave her a proper greeting as she deserved. I was taught a very important lesson through this and tried not to repeat any similar lack of manners.

If you are living in the country, it is quite common that you will be allocated a Ugandan name yourself. This occurred when I was training a group of head teachers. They chose the name Kisakye for me which means 'Grace' and I was very happy with this name choice.

The language of the Baganda tribe is called Luganda. (An individual native is called a Muganda and the plural is Buganda.) I learnt a few phrases of Luganda but was fortunate that nearly everyone spoke English. The pupils in our school were not supposed to speak to each other using their local language but always to use English. I was quite taken aback during one break-time, when a young pupil ran into my office to tell me indignantly that, 'Joshua is using the vernacular, Miss!' I had to stop and think for a moment just what he meant, but I did not consider the 'crime' warranted discipline. I was also confused the first time a girl reported that, 'Samuel is abusing me, Miss Holly.' Further investigations revealed that this was a phrase used for minor teasing and not the type of behaviour that had been conjured up in my mind.

Running Together

I have never been particularly sporty, although in recent years I have enjoyed some running, alongside the nearby River Thames. I do enjoy watching athletes run in competitions and was particularly impressed with the Kenyan runners in the 2012 Olympics. It was noticeable that when an individual Kenyan won a race, any other Kenyans who had also raced participated in the lap of honour around the stadium. Despite the competitive element, this was now a team victory and they were all happy to share in the victory celebration.

I saw a similar attitude with my friends in Uganda. When a young person graduates with a diploma or degree, not only does the immediate family celebrate but the whole community celebrates too. There is an understanding and appreciation of the effort, cost and commitment undertaken to reach this milestone. Such a financial cost is a huge burden on one family so the wider family also contributes where it can. In this extended family, cousins can be referred to as sons and daughters, and even family friends become known as aunty or uncle. The African proverb is very relevant here: 'It takes a village to raise a child.'

In our Western society, we are expected to carry our own financial burdens or the state provides for those who are unable to do this. In Uganda, generally, money is not saved for the future. The future is unpredictable, therefore money is best spent immediately. There would be no funds set aside for a son's or daughter's engagement, known as 'introduction', or later for their actual wedding. For such functions, a large financial outlay is the norm. It is traditional for three to four hundred people to attend such ceremonies. The venue, food, entertainment and outfits amount to a large cost. The solution is found in everybody making a contribution. A wedding list is printed of the itemised requirements and the cost of each one. This includes clothes, flowers, seating, tents, food, drink, dancers, decoration and every other necessity for a successful wedding ceremony. It is usual for there to be about eight or nine bridesmaids and sometimes two best men. Outfits are hired and they are usually bright, colourful and flamboyant. Family and friends receive the wedding list and agree to cover the cost of particular items. A committee of close friends is appointed and they are responsible for monitoring the budget and forthcoming income. I was invited to one of these meetings when a member of our Wellspring church was getting married. I discovered that every contribution, however small or large, was read out and applauded by the committee. They then encouraged each other to work hard to gather more contributions as everybody wanted the very best for the occasion.

It surprised me that sometimes the introduction would be held in the same month as the wedding, thereby presenting two expensive events concurrently. The introduction is as vital traditionally as the wedding ceremony because it is where the two families are introduced to each other. The groom's family brings a whole range of gifts to present to the bride's family. The gifts may include sacks of sugar, chickens, fabrics, clothing or even a cow. During the event, it is usual for the bride to appear in three or four different outfits.

I was always a welcome member of the party and I enjoyed wearing the traditional Buganda dress known as a gomez. Such dresses on the ladies look so spectacular and bring an impressive ambience to any celebration.

Africa: Birthright and Calling

PART FOUR

Detours

If you want to go fast, go alone. If you want to go far, go together.

African proverb

A snail's pace.

Police Palaver

Driving from Bweyogerere to Kampala is quite an experience. Most visitors I took there felt they would never be confident enough to drive that journey. I absolutely loved it, despite the traffic jams, floods, hawkers and potholes: they made it all the more interesting and challenging. As you approach town, street sellers stand on the central reservation, eyeing you up as a potential customer. A small shake of your head signifies you are not interested, and they usually pass to another vehicle. I would often have a 2000 shilling note ready to buy the newspaper. If I offered a note of 5000, they would return 2000 back to me and then pause. I would then remind them I needed another 1000 and that I was not an unsuspecting tourist but lived nearby. Their faces would break into big beaming smiles as we shared a little humour and banter before moving on. Street sellers stand in the heat and dust all day selling a few wares, and any little extra helps out, so I never begrudged their efforts to top up their money this way. They certainly provide interest as you wait at the traffic lights and observe a medley of sweets, cushions, toys, flannels and wall pictures for sale.

Every third vehicle, at least, is a Toyota minibus known as a taxi, which is used to ferry passengers to and from Kampala and to farther destinations. The drivers hardly ever signal but just suddenly pull into the side, stopping to collect more passengers. You learn to anticipate their actions and drive accordingly. All drivers who want to arrive somewhere must drive very close to the bumper of the car in front; otherwise, any space given will be taken by weaving motorcycles that dodge continually through the traffic. Time is money for them. The system of driving could not be replicated here in England, but there, it mainly works and few collisions occur. It is out on the more open roads, where the taxis drive excessively fast, that serious accidents happen, injuring and killing many. Most taxis display a slogan or motto on the back window. These usually show adherence to a faith, football team or way of life. When you see 'Oh, my God', 'Pray Harder' or 'God will get you there', you appreciate that divine protection together with a sense of humour may be what is needed when using this transport system.

Driving through an area of Kampala on one occasion, I was warned by the police to drive out of the area, as protests involving stones being thrown at vehicles had just occurred. I then noticed large stones around the pavements and gutters and quickly moved into a safer area. Another time, I entered Kampala quite early in the morning and passed a dead body on the side of the road. Pedestrians were passing by on their way to work, presuming that at some point it would be collected by a police van.

One of the amazing sights as you travelled was the variety of objects that could be carried by passengers on a motorcycle, known as a boda-boda. Nothing is a surprise once you have seen a sofa, large television, huge plate of glass, a breastfeeding mother, a goat, a bed and various other large items carried in this way. Knowing how often passengers have fallen from these bikes, I feared for the person as well as the valuable item they were transporting. To save money, whole families would take one boda-boda, two in front of the driver and four or more clinging on behind. I myself enjoyed going on the bikes but only around Bweyogerere where I knew the trustworthy riders. On a hot day, it is the best way to cool down as the breeze wafts over you while you weave in and out between cars, people or animals. It is customary for female riders to sit side-saddle, so you remain secure by clinging onto the small luggage rack behind. As I was older and white, most riders would kindly steer carefully around the bigger potholes, which I always appreciated.

Most Saturday mornings, I drove to town for essential supplies as well as for shopping therapy and a good café to enjoy a morning coffee. Traffic police are on the lookout for reprobates to stop, and they spotted me easily as a white person. The first time I saw a policeman waving me to the side of the road, I felt confused as I knew I had done nothing wrong and my vehicle was fully legal. I was silently observed through my open window and I waited while my Rav 4 was inspected as well as my insurance certificate on the back window. Then, having checked my licence, without any further conversation, he waved me to move on again. With a rush of relief and adrenalin, I headed for the nearest coffee shop for a strong dose of caffeine to calm my nerves.

I soon adopted a different response when I found myself being stopped regularly. Instead of looking like a guilty, scared culprit, I offered a cheerful greeting and calmly passed my licence for inspection. I now understood that police pay is very poor and every effort is required to top up the salary, particularly at the start of term when school fees are due. It is a part of life here, where a small side-payment could be offered to avoid a lengthy and expensive official police prosecution. Over the coming years, I had several amusing and challenging encounters with the police which I would be asked to relate at staff parties for their entertainment.

The resort of Jinja became my favourite place to visit during a weekend or school holiday. At the end of our road, the main Jinja Road led to Kampala on the right and Jinja on the left. Whenever I turned left, it gave me a sense of freedom, adventure and joy as I set towards the open road that led through beautiful countryside and small trading estates. Along the roadside were sellers offering fruit, vegetables, charcoal or crafts, all exhibited on small wooden stalls. Baboons were usually spotted through the forest before the road opened out to fields of tall sugar cane and then farther on to tea estates. Children would wave as you passed their small homesteads interspersed by banana trees, flowering blossom and small animals wandering around. As you approach Jinja you see the dam, opened in 1953 by Princess Elizabeth, then cross the bridge over the River Nile which winds below, travelling its way north towards the Mediterranean Sea, 4000 miles away. Massive advertising boards display Ugandan Nile beer brewed in this area and enjoyed nationally. The town architecture has a colonial style and side roads reveal stunning examples of Indian architecture with balconies, turrets and garden fountains, most now sadly in ruins.

Driving home after my first visit to Jinja, a lorry stalled as it came to the start of the bridge running alongside the dam. I saw the opportunity to lean through the window and get a good photograph of the dam. In fact, beside the dam itself, I had photographed the policeman waving at me. He moved over to explain that security measures prohibited the taking of photos in the area. After expressing my ignorance, regret and apologies, he waved me on as by now the traffic was piling up behind. The team at Wellspring were amazed that I was not prosecuted and couldn't believe that my charm had allowed me to escape a serious fine.

Friends, who were visiting me from England, wanted to see Jinja when I told them all that it offered. We decided to hire a good quality vehicle for the journey instead of using the saloon car I had at the time. The morning of our departure, I received a phone call from George who was hiring me a Rav 4 that I had previously inspected. Unfortunately, it was no longer available, he explained. Another voice came on the line and offered me his vehicle to hire at the same price. When it was delivered, it was in no way comparable to the vehicle I had wanted and I retained a large amount of the cost as a precaution. The windscreen had a massive crack through the middle, as well as a crack on the side mirror. It had no petrol and no oil for the engine. However, we finally set off and enjoyed the wonderful drive out to Jinja.

We drove for a meal to a place in Jinja I knew well, intending to move later to the hotel I had booked for the weekend. I returned to the vehicle to retrieve something I needed to pass to the manageress here and found the boot was unlocked. When I looked inside, I was horrified and shocked. There was nothing, it was completely empty. All our cases, bags, camera, PC were gone. Calling to my friends, they too stood in shock and dismay. We knew we had definitely locked the boot.

We had chosen deliberately to park in a secure, guarded site that catered for Western tourists and was well-known in the area. As we had driven into the parking area, we had noticed the armed watchman at the gate entrance. Now he was nowhere to be seen. I was furious and stormed through the gardens looking for him, where I found him loitering near some rubbish, and expressed my anger. At this point, the acting manageress, a non-Ugandan, appeared slowly from her cottage where she had been resting during a break. Her hostile and sarcastic attitude was not appreciated but she did call the police for us. The district officer asked some questions and then asked us to follow him to the police station. Here we were asked to write out statements about the robbery. It took a while for paper and pens to be located for us to use and by then darkness had come down and a small candle on a saucer was lit for us as power was off that evening. Several people put their heads in at the doorway to see some mzungus who had been robbed. We began to list all our missing possessions but it became like a game show when one of us would suddenly cry out, 'oh, nightwear' or 'swimming gear' and 'oh no, new binoculars', as if these items were on a revolving conveyor belt inside our memories. The worst realization was that due to the security provision of the place, my friends had left passports, dollars and sterling inside the vehicle also.

By now the atmosphere was quite friendly. The policeman on duty introduced us to his wife who arrived with his cooked supper on a tray. The manageress had softened her manner and wanted to be sympathetic and helpful. Inviting us back to her hotel for that night, she agreed to cancel our other booking. We returned there, said goodnight and went to our respective rooms. I woke in the morning, on my own in a strange room with nothing but the clothes I had worn the previous day and a complimentary toothbrush with toothpaste. It was a desolate and disorientating feeling.

Such vulnerability and shock you feel at these times is quite hard to process. We met for breakfast together and then began the drive back home to contact the embassy in Kampala for temporary passports. These were urgently needed as my friends were leaving for a safari on the Monday morning and their passports would be necessary.

Fortunately, this was my worst experience in Uganda and nobody was hurt or damaged in any way. We had only lost material possessions, most of which could be replaced. I still regard Jinja as my favourite place in Uganda and when I pass the police station on the main through-road, I smile and remember our candlelit evening inside.

Sometimes it appears that everyone needs a small break. One lady police officer hitched a lift with me for a tea and snack back at base, as I later realized. She waved me to stop and said there was something wrong with my vehicle. She wanted it checked at the nearby police post and proceeded to get into the front passenger seat. Farther down the road, I signalled left and began to turn in towards the place but she stopped me, explaining that she had just wanted a lift back there and everything was fine! With a smile and a wave, she left me to turn into the traffic again.

Farther into town, near Lugogo, where many road police hover, I was stopped another time. All the routine things were checked and I was wondering what the problem could be. The policeman then asked where I worked, so I said Wellspring. A huge smile spread across his face. 'Wellspring, Wellspring, you work at Wellspring. What a wonderful place, my wife had her firstborn there. They were so good to her. Off you go and you have a good day now.'

The most persistence I experienced in trying to obtain money from me as a bribe was along the Kololo Road. I had not put on my seatbelt as I reversed from the surgery after collecting a prescription. I was spotted immediately and followed on a boda by a young policeman who overtook me and signalled for me to stop. I admitted that I had put on the seatbelt quickly when I saw him. He explained that as a consequence I would need to attend court and be given a fine. A small sum of money though could avoid this predicament. I was not willing to offer him any money in this way and he was most surprised at my non-cooperation. He tried to persuade me by warning me that I could spend the day at court, totally disorganising my day and how I could so easily avoid that with just a little money. As I still refused, he asked me to follow him to the nearest police station and we set off towards the main road. Near the bottom of the hill, he pulled into the side and signalled for me to do the same. At my window, he made a last attempt to abstract some money but finally realized he was wasting his time. Now smiling at me he said, 'Well, go on, this time I will forgive you. Off you go.' I waved goodbye cheerfully and with my seatbelt firmly fastened, I headed to the Good Coffee Shop to relax and smile to myself.

I have to admit that on two other occasions, I was not so fortunate. The first time I was fined for overtaking on the new bypass bridge. Then, just days before I left Uganda finally to return home, a cheerful policeman discovered that the tread on my tyres was not an acceptable depth. I had already agreed a sale for the Rav but now I had a fine to pay and tyres to fix. Well, maybe I was really a true Ugandan now after all!

Found Them

When I was growing up in a family of six, we were often all involved in a frantic hunt for my mother's lost keys. We all knew that she had just mislaid them somewhere nearby but we duly responded to the crisis and ran around the house until we heard the shout, 'I've found them!' Similarly, during my time at Wellspring there was often a small crisis when various keys went missing and a hunt would begin. Each teacher had to hang their class key at the end of the day on a board in the school office. Many mornings a class and their teacher were not able to enter the classroom because the key was missing. The blame was usually put onto the maintenance team or the cleaner, never the teacher themselves. Quite often it would be found in their coat pocket or had been left in another room by mistake. A lot of frustration could build up as time was wasted by such incidents. However, I had to admit that I had my own difficulties with keys on occasion.

I lived at first in a compound owned by the Wellspring director and his wife, Mike and Beryl. They owned two adjoining houses with an interlinking office block in between. We each appreciated our own space and privacy but enjoyed spending time at the end of a day in the garden with a relaxing drink. Each year, Mike and Beryl would return to England for two months, so I would be on my own in the large compound. Usually, in the mornings, Mike unlocked and opened the big entrance gates for me to exit and drive to work. When he was away, I needed to manoeuvre them myself. I am never at my best in the early morning, so my brain just goes into automatic pilot to perform routine tasks.

One morning, I opened the gates, drove my Rav through to the other side and parked it with the engine running while I locked the gates before leaving. Inadvertently, I went inside and locked the gates from inside the compound as you do when returning in the evening, having just driven your vehicle inside. This was the morning though. I had reversed the process. The key to open the padlock I had just locked was hanging on my bunch of keys in the ignition of my vehicle, alongside my bag, phone and PC! This could not be happening. I might wait all day inside here with no food, no water and no way of contacting anyone. I could not even re-enter my own home, it was all locked up. I went into crisis mode immediately and knelt down on the concrete in front of the gates. This was not for prayer. I began to call out at the small opening through which you squeeze your hand to lock or open the padlock. I could see the legs of people as they passed by but nobody stopped to help. A child looked through the gap but ran off when he saw a white face staring at him.

Eventually, after much calling out, a lovely face appeared in the gap and asked me what was wrong. 'Please, I need your help as I am locked in here by mistake. That vehicle running outside belongs to me and my keys are there in the ignition. I need you to get them for me and pass them through this gap so I can unlock the padlock to get out.' Well, that is exactly what he did. A beautiful black hand reached through the gap and passed me my keys. I got out and locked the gates behind me just as the young man was riding away on a boda to head to work. 'Thank you, thank you so much!' I called out as he waved and rode off, wondering, I am sure, how a crazy white lady could lock herself inside like that. I jumped into my driving seat and felt so thankful when I saw all my belongings still on the passenger seat where I had left them.

Shifty Business

When someone tells you they are 'shifting', it means they are moving to a new house. After four years of living in one home, I was shifting to a new one. The Wellspring directors, Mike and Beryl, were shifting to South Africa so I needed to find a new place to rent for accommodation. I viewed a couple of places, but they were not suitable from a security perspective. We then heard about a house available to rent which was right next door to Wellspring.

I was warned it might be far too big for my purposes but as soon as I entered it, I knew this needed to be my next home. It had a lot of interest and character in the architecture of the building with attractive Gothic-style security grilles at each window and a large verandah overlooking a big garden. From the garage attached at the side of the house, there were steps to a higher verandah. This looked out across the valley and fields where cows grazed and our football team played their games. I had so wanted a house with a view. At night, the lights twinkled in the homes across the slopes, and the sunrise and sunset views were beautiful from this height. The house had such potential, despite it being then just an empty shell.

In negotiations with the landlord, we agreed that the necessary work on the house could be done and financed by me. To make it suitable to rent to a Western individual or family, he knew it needed a lot of work. My home church lent me the money and I lived rent free until all my expenses had been covered. The landlord thereby had the benefit of a house fully developed to a high standard with no financial outlay involved. Everything had to be built, fitted, painted or secured. I was able to choose the paint colour for both inner and outer walls, select the tiles, design the cupboards for the kitchen and bedrooms, and the landlord even allowed a side entrance to be made so I could access Wellspring directly. A relationship of goodwill and trust was built between the landlord and me. I was left to supervise the work though, and this was quite an experience.

Although we had set a completion date, work moved on very slowly. Subcontractors began work and then disappeared altogether while others began but took a break from the job for a week at a time. Paint tins were left to drip on the concrete floors, the sink was damaged and new tiles laid in the toilet and bathroom had small cracks. When I pointed out these concerns, it was always the responsibility of another workman. 'I'm not the one,' was the usual response if blame was to be avoided. Being a single female on my own, it was not easy handling the whole project myself. To speed up the work, I decided to move in, even though the house was not yet ready. I would then be on site and able, hopefully, to help bring the work to a conclusion.

The only usable room was the garage, so that is where I found all my possessions piled up by the removal men who had shifted me from one home to the next. Everything had been loaded onto an open truck and deposited in the garage before I had been able to arrive myself. I managed to clear items from the bed so I could make it up for that night. Some nights I needed to clamber over furniture and boxes to visit the bathroom. This was harder when the power was off and I felt my way in the dark. Returning to my bed one night, I tripped and an upright table leg jabbed into my ribs. I hobbled into work the next morning wishing the workers would finish soon. In the meantime, a relative of the landlord kept passing by to try to persuade me to retain their guard dog which was still in its kennel in the garden. All along I had stated I absolutely did not want this dog to remain.

Finally, we reached a day when the work was completed and I was able to unpack and settle properly into my new home. Somehow though, I still had the dog! The relatives did then arrange for a vet to visit the house. He was horrified at the aggressive and violent behaviour of this dog. He was not able to approach it at all to inject it and sadly it received an alternative end that was horrifying and distressing for the animal. I was so relieved when it was wheeled away from my house in a wheelbarrow. It seemed some fleas must have escaped as I found a few jumping when I sat on the sofa at night. Fortunately, they soon disappeared, but were replaced with small rats scuttling across the floor. A friend investigated and found that a nest had been made in the back of my sofa, which he covered with wire to avoid this in future. Fleas and rats dealt with, I hoped I could now relax on my sofa.

I became accustomed to a variety of wildlife entering my home. Some did not give any concern, such as the tiny jumping spiders, the sweet little geckos and even the cockroaches that could be eliminated easily by spraying them with Doom. I did not like flying animals entering though and felt quite unsettled when a black bat suddenly flew across the room as I watched television one evening. It settled behind the sofa and was extricated by the night watchman. I also discovered that some cockroaches could fly and that was not pleasant at all. Small frogs sometimes made their presence known by jumping suddenly near your feet and at night these made a racket outside my window when they mated in the moonlight.

A month before returning to England, I was visited by a black mamba. I was returning to my house late one evening and saw it on the drain outside my back door. It was fortunate the power was on, else I would not have seen it there. When I called to the watchman, he was most hesitant and reluctant to respond. Eventually, the nurse on duty at the health centre helped persuade him and she gave him a long stick to use instead of the flimsy branch he had picked from a bush. To my amazement and huge relief, the snake had not moved away during this time and it was soon killed and deposited onto my rubbish heap where I observed it the next day. I went inside, made a nice cup of tea and retired to bed. When I think of the number of times I got ready for bed in the dark when the power was off, I wonder what could have been around my house then. Ignorance was bliss!

Having settled into my new home, I wanted to put up some pictures on the walls. Innocent, our maintenance man, offered to help me after work one evening. Our last task before he left was to put some material at my bedroom windows as I had no curtains there. I stood on a stool to assist and reached to point out where the nail should go. The next moment I was crashing onto the concrete floor where I groaned in pain with a strangely deformed wrist. I was actually howling with pain and poor Innocent tried to take that hand to help me up from the floor. 'Don't touch it,' I wailed when he tried a second time. He then realized that help was needed and ran to the health centre next door at Wellspring. From this point on, I became the centre of everyone's attention. I remember Nurse Gaudi trying to encourage me by saying, 'Take heart, Miss Holly, take heart.' She then injected my behind with a huge injection to help ease the pain. Gradually, more and more people arrived in my bedroom. Two teachers living close by wanted to help, a patient in the health centre decided the scene was worth observing, a couple of nurses attended and throughout my ordeal, Innocent hovered, wringing his hands in worry. My good friend Amos arrived, having been alerted to the problem, and it was decided that he would drive me to the hospital in Kampala using my vehicle. Anyone who has had experience of the Ugandan roads knows how bumpy they are. Clutching my poor arm, I pleaded with Amos to go slower, but he told me he was going as slowly as he possibly could. By midnight, it was confirmed that I had broken my wrist in two places and would go to theatre in the morning. Herbert and Eve, as directors of Wellspring, had been contacted and they arrived at the hospital late, as they had spent the whole evening trying to locate the necessary funding for the hospital fees. About two thousand pounds was required before any treatment could begin, so arrangements with insurers and lenders of money were necessary.

In the morning, when I informed the surgeon that I was a good pianist, he decided to put a plate into the wrist. I had my operation and returned on a drip. No food is provided by the hospital but Eve had arranged for juice and snacks to be brought to me by one of our office staff. That evening, Jacky arrived to spend the night with me, help me get to the bathroom and generally take good care of me in my new predicament. We developed a special relationship through this and laughed about it afterwards. When I left to go home with my arm in plaster, Jacky spent the first night with me. It was hard to sleep and I cushioned my arm on a pillow to get some relief. The next six weeks were not easy trying to dress, wash clothes and shower using just one arm. I could not drive either so my freedom was curtailed. This was still only my first month in my new home, but unbeknown to me, more disasters were occurring in my own house back in England.

My first tenant had given two months' notice to end the contract, and the managing agent for the property interviewed new tenants, who took up the tenancy and paid the first month's rent as expected. Subsequently, the rent ceased being paid and the agent contacted a friend of mine to investigate the situation. It transpired that instead of three people living in the house, there had been at least thirteen – all illegal immigrants. Somehow, they had been tipped off, as when my friend entered the house, on the table were half-finished plates of food, the house was full of all their possessions and the police were making investigations into a stolen car. There were sleeping bags on the floor downstairs, bunkbeds upstairs and even a passport had been left in the haste to vacate the building.

Eight ladies from church spent eight hours sorting through all the items in the house and allocating them either to the bin, refuse dump or charity shop. I had left my house fully furnished and equipped with all necessary household items. Most had to be discarded as they were no longer fit for purpose. When all had been cleared and the house professionally cleaned, I was informed of the situation. I was just about to return for the Christmas break so, as I had no tenant, I decided to stay in the house myself while I was in England. However, when I returned to Uganda, I still had not found a tenant so for six months I had no income. I had cancelled the managing agency after this trouble and a good friend offered to manage the house for me as her way of supporting my voluntary work in Uganda. By reducing the monthly rent, she managed to obtain a reliable new tenant and I was relieved to have income going into my account regularly once more. Fortunately, all subsequent tenants took good care of my home, for which I was grateful, as I knew that at some stage I would be returning to live there once more myself.

PART FIVE

Landmarks

We're on the World Stage.[9]

Norman Barnes
Founder of Links International

First training cohort of head teachers

---

[9] Norman Barnes, Founder of Links International

TGIF

Alongside my work in the school, I initiated activities for various groups of people. I regularly invited a group of young girls to my home on Saturday afternoons. During this time, we chatted, laughed a lot, played games and generally got to know each other. They especially enjoyed doing craftwork and cooking. We made flapjacks, cookies and a variety of muffins. Most were eaten as soon as they were cool, but usually a small sample for the family went home at the end.

Friends of mine at work, though secure in a steady job, did not have spare income for entertainment outside of the home. I decided to bring the office ladies together each Friday when we had finished work. I called the group TGIF representing 'Thank God It's Friday'! Though a familiar phrase in England, it was not known in Uganda. With our desks clear, we would leave the office and head over to my home where I had sodas and snacks prepared. Sitting on the cool verandah, we relaxed together, chatting and sharing stories. Old *Hello* magazines caused fun as we compared and commented on the glamorous outfits worn by the stars. All African ladies love glamour and style, taking great care and pride in their hairstyles, nail decorations and colourful outfits. In my opinion, their short-cropped hair displayed their beautiful facial features to the best. They, however, admire our longer windswept styles and many ladies wear wigs of different lengths and colours. Their patience is endless when they spend eight hours at a salon having braids or weaves skilfully added. We enjoyed beginning our weekend together, discussing light-hearted subjects and generally developing our friendships.

At special times of the year, I enjoyed organising events for the ladies in our church. We all dressed in our best and gathered together in my home where little needed to be organised beyond the refreshments and decorations. Very soon, lively individuals would have everyone singing, dancing or playing fun, competitive team games. Food would be enjoyed together and we felt happy in sharing our friendship, love and laughter this way. One Christmas, they were intrigued by the chocolate logs I presented to them. I explained that in England, we always hoped it would snow on Christmas Day and that the icing sugar dusted over the logs represented the snow. Having never experienced snow, they could not imagine us wanting it to be so cold. On a mildly hot day, they would often comment on how cold it was. It was not cold at all compared to our British weather. I would still be wearing sleeveless tops while they huddled in thick cardigans or jackets.

When I was queuing to check in at Heathrow airport one time, I stood behind a lady carrying a violin case. She noticed I had a flute case in my hand luggage and we soon began to chat. It transpired that she had founded the Kampala Music School and was returning to visit there. Through her contact, I was able to join a choir there and every Tuesday evening I drove to Kampala for choir rehearsals. We had a mixture of Ugandans and other nationalities of people working with the government or in non-governmental organisations. We performed concerts in the Anglican cathedral, which is a stunning building high on a hill with a view right across Kampala. The music of Vivaldi, Rutter and Purcell resounded through the arches and lifted the spirits of both performers and audience. I also began flute lessons with the director of the Music School but found the heat and the high altitude quite a hindrance to breathing sufficiently. Nevertheless, on a Saturday my neighbours could hear my attempts as I practised simple children's songs.

One lady at choir told me about the 'Kampala Sale', held once a month in the Makindi district. This became my monthly treat and I attended whenever I could. It was held at the American Recreation Centre, so we had to pass through strict security to enter the grounds where stalls were laid out with wares for sale. Many African crafts, jewellery and artefacts would be on sale and some stalls sold second-hand clothes. The stalls I became most keen to visit were the ones run by expatriates as they were selling items from their homes before leaving the country, having finished their terms of employment. I found some fantastic items to buy each time I went. My house was being cheaply furnished and equipped this way and it was greatly admired by visitors.

At these sales I met very interesting people from America, Russia, Denmark and the Netherlands. Across the months we got to know each other and met for coffee after our purchasing. It was fun seeing what everyone had bought and good to meet and spend time with people outside of Wellspring. When it was my own turn to leave Uganda, I also had a stall on several occasions. I loved all the treasures I had collected over the years but I had to be realistic and practical: my house in England was far smaller than the one I had been enjoying in Uganda.

Church Matters

After working all week and getting up early in the mornings, I really valued and appreciated a lie-in on Saturdays and Sundays. Living next to Wellspring, I would be woken at about 8.30am on Sundays when the band began to practise for the morning service. I accepted this happily but was not so keen if the music began around 7.00am. Whenever this happened, I would jump out of bed, pull on my dressing gown and march crossly over to the hall. It would often be an individual who wanted to play and listen to loud music rather than sit bored at home. I made it very clear in my head teacher manner that this was not acceptable to me or to nearby neighbours. The culprit would look at me sheepishly and turn down the music, and I would march my way back again. Later at the church meeting, I would give that person a reassuring grin to signal we were still friends. They would smile to themselves knowing Miss Holly did not 'mince her words'.

The music for any event or party is always set at full volume, the louder the better. Some parties would continue until at least 5.00am at weekends and you had to try to sleep through the noise. If there were any noise and environment laws, nobody in our area seemed to observe them. It is not surprising that when my friends from Uganda visit and stay in my home in England, they comment on the peace and quiet.

The church services we attended on a Sunday morning brought us together as a church family. Everyone dressed smartly, with ladies wearing very colourful, bright African outfits and men wearing suits or at least smart trousers with shirt and tie. The services were long, the heat could be soporific, but the loud music and shouting into the microphone kept your attention. There was often dancing to the songs and I always participated with enthusiasm and energy. Africans tend to consider Westerners poor dancers who just side-step on the spot and show no rhythm. They appreciated my lively dancing though, and I found it easy to copy their steps and movements. At special wedding or graduation celebrations, visitors would comment favourably on seeing the mzungu enjoying the local dances and traditions.

Children from a really young age can dance the movements too and this natural sense of rhythm seems innate. At church, they joined in cheerfully and behaved themselves throughout the length of the service. They are expected to sit quietly and still from the youngest age and do not demand attention or become restless. It is good to be aware of how they are expected to behave, otherwise visitors might engage young children in playing with them during the service or try to amuse them, which would be distracting to those sitting nearby. After the meeting is over, they will love to surround you, have their photo taken and enjoy interacting.

It is worth knowing that some adults appear at church when they hear a 'white team' is visiting. They see an opportunity to flatter and befriend you hoping to make a financial gain. Our regular church members would not behave in this way. Their friendliness is genuine and real and a Ugandan welcome is all-embracing and loving. To avoid passing money unwisely, visitors are encouraged not to give money to an individual. If a pressing problem is seen and causing concern, it is best to mention it to the leadership so that a gift can be allocated centrally and administered carefully by them. When people have little, it is extremely easy to become jealous of others. Even offering small items as gifts can make some feel neglected and left out if it is done in a public place. Again, such items can be left with the leader of the organisation to distribute evenly and fairly. It is always natural to want to thank and bless those with whom we have spent some time, but a little forethought can avoid resentment or jealousy after visitors have left.

I sometimes received written requests for financial help and on one occasion, a letter was pushed under our gate 'for the attention of the Irish lady'. Mike presumed that meant me. It was written by someone I did not know and had never met. He had listed about fifty items he required for the forthcoming birth of his baby and encouraged me in the letter to bless him in this way, because I would then be greatly blessed in return. Such letters did not pull at my heartstrings and went straight into the bin!

Obviously, I was very rich in comparison with my neighbours. The many items you owned such as cars, houses and modern utensils that made life easier, these all displayed your wealth. In reality, the rent I received from my house in England was my only income and covered only the basic costs of my expenses there and in Uganda. In England, I needed to fund management and legal fees, maintenance and repair bills and gardening costs. In Uganda, I had my rent to pay plus all the utilities, cleaning, furnishing, maintenance and gardening costs as well as food, living and medical expenses, petrol and a monthly tithe. On top of that, I needed to reserve a significant sum to cover the costly flights home at least once a year.

After my second year of driving a saloon car, my home church felt a safer, sturdier vehicle would be advisable as I was travelling mostly on my own. A church appeal raised a large sum towards this. My bank balance suddenly increased and this had been noticed. The whole amount disappeared as fast as it was entered. Fortunately, it was reimbursed by my bank but then it happened again straight away. Somebody had forged my signature and a cheque travelled to China in my name. The fraud squad in England were involved and again I was reimbursed and able finally to buy a very smart Rav 4 which I treasured and loved driving.

Another time, when I was using an ATM machine to obtain cash, it kept refusing to dispense any. I tried various other branches and the same thing happened, so I was forced to borrow cash for a time. It was months later I discovered that nearly £1,000 had gone out from my account in these transactions, but I had received none of this money. When I was back in England, I was informed by the bank that too much time had elapsed for me to claim this back.

Fortunately, I had made a firm decision as regards money before I left to travel to Uganda: any costs that were incurred in living there were fully my responsibility even though I was doing voluntary work. I would not allow the issue of money, whether it was stolen from me, lost or misplaced, to cause a stumbling block. This kept my spirit strong and peaceful in some quite difficult circumstances. I was able to live well and be generous to others around me. I was rich beyond measure and grateful for all I had.

World Stage

When I was in England visiting family and friends, I often met people who were very surprised by what I was doing. 'Isn't it a bit dangerous in Uganda?' they would ask. Many people still remembered news reports from the seventies when Idi Amin overthrew the Obote government and a time of terror and death enveloped the country. Obote had destroyed the royal palaces of the Kabaka, the King who heads the Buganda kingdom. When Edward Mutessa, the current Kabaka, had to flee to London at a young age, he spent time at Christian camps with Paul, a good friend of mine. Paul and his wife visited me in 2006 in Uganda and we contacted the Kabaka's office. Paul's grandfather had been one of the early Christian missionaries in Uganda and had worked for a time at the university in Mukono. Paul himself had inherited the most amazing photo album which has wonderful sepia photos of the Kabaka in younger days. This would be of great interest now, as by destroying the palaces, Obote had destroyed all artefacts and photographs of special events that were now of historical interest.

One morning, the phone in the office rang. Imagine our administrator's amazement and excitement when she learnt it was the Kabaka himself asking to speak to Paul! They chatted for a while and recalled times past that they had shared. An invitation was offered to go that week to the palace and meet the Kabaka. Sadly, Paul was flying home the next day, so a meeting could not be arranged. It would have been such a special opportunity.

More recent atrocities in the history of Uganda now lodge in people's minds, having seen images on television of child soldiers and young night commuters fleeing soldiers of the so-called 'Lord's Army'. One of my teachers explained to me that as a young teenager she had lived near Gulu, where the trouble there was causing the young people and children to walk into large towns every night to keep safe from marauding soldiers in her village. In the mornings, they had to walk all the way back to attend school. Other friends described hiding under their school desks when soldiers entered the area. The country had experienced such traumatic times and many people in the UK still connected those images to Uganda. However, the government under Museveni has brought stability to the country again. The economy is developing and infrastructures are improving. This has not given benefit to everyone though, and many tribal and regional jealousies still persist and stir tensions across the country, particularly in the northern parts.

The country was described by Winston Churchill as the 'Pearl of Africa'. Pearls hold significant value and the greatest asset in Uganda – the pearls – is its own people. The Ugandans I came to love and respect are willing to work hard, take risks and be imaginative in order to provide for their families. Nevertheless, opportunities are lacking for many, as the majority of people live on a subsistence level, growing food to provide for the family and selling the little they have over to purchase other provisions. Life becomes a battle for survival when poverty surrounds you and you can find no way of breaking free.

Uganda is a land-locked country, surrounded by six other countries. The transportation of people and goods has to rely on a road system that is not maintained well by the government. Potholes are plentiful and road safety is scant and unpredictable. The airport at Entebbe receives a high number of tourists, many people coming to work and help the country develop further, and sometimes even royalty.

During 2007, the government was preparing to host the Common-wealth Conference. The road from the airport to Kampala was improved and the capital itself received a facelift. Sites were built or developed to accommodate the delegates and there was a general atmosphere of excitement and anticipation. Sadly, the financial arrangements were tarnished by claims of corruption. When I returned to Uganda for a visit seven years later, in 2014, I found newspapers were still reporting on ongoing investigations. Despite this, Queen Elizabeth II arrived from London in 2007 to open the conference and give her support to the Commonwealth and particularly Uganda as hosts. Security was on high alert.

Nearing the start of the conference, I was working at my desk in school when suddenly I heard a loud explosion and saw several people running towards the health centre. As I ran to the hall, I could see blood on the ground and splattered on the walls. One of our young men had received a package. It had been collected from the postbox in town and when he opened it he found a pen inside which he passed to a nearby member of staff. As this person removed the pen lid, there was a small explosion which damaged his hand and fingers. Everyone was shocked by this incident and very soon the police arrived on site collecting information and details. The postbox and the main post office were close to the venue where the opening ceremony for the conference was being held. This incident alarmed the security personnel who were responsible for the safety of everyone for this event. We were immediately provided with an armed security guard at the entrance gates and this was maintained throughout the time the conference was in progress. Fortunately, there were no other incidents. We did feel vulnerable for a time though, and took extra safety precautions.

Towards the end of the conference week, the Duke and Duchess of Cornwall, Charles and Camilla, made a trip to Jinja. Late on the Saturday afternoon, I walked to the main road to buy a newspaper, where I found crowds gathered there and a policeman explained to me that the royal motorcade was passing by shortly on its return from Jinja to Kampala. I pushed my way to the front, and was so excited and waved enthusiastically when Charles and Camilla drove right past the end of my road. They must have noticed me as I was the only white person in the crowd there at Bweyogerere. I walked back home and told Mike and Beryl how I had just waved to Charles and Camilla but unfortunately they were not able to stop for a cup of tea with us. Despite the accusations of corruption that surrounded the organisation of the conference, the event was a great success for Uganda. The country had delivered a safe, valuable and enjoyable time for all the visiting delegates. I was proud of Uganda.

Jinja itself is a very popular destination for most visitors to Uganda, not just royal ones. It lies to the east of Kampala and boasts a famous national site. Back in 1856, two explorers, Richard Francis Burton and John Hanning Speke, set off on a geographical expedition based around the lakes, mountains and River Nile in this part of Uganda. They had set off from the East African coast, trying to find the source of the Nile. They had to face many hostilities on the way including dangerous swamps, severe diseases, unreliable porters as well as resistant tribes and chiefs. Burton became seriously ill and it was decided that Speke would continue alone. He discovered a huge lake which he thought was the source of the Nile River. He was in Tanzania at the time and he named it Lake Victoria after the British Queen. Lake Victoria is the biggest lake in Africa and provides employment and food for all its surrounding communities.

Because Burton placed doubt on his findings, Speke set off again in 1860. For two years he trekked through difficult terrain facing many problems and disappointments. When he arrived at some waterfalls, he stood on the bank and felt sure he was standing by the beginning of the Nile. He named the falls the Ripon Falls and claimed that these were the start of the river's long journey to the Mediterranean Sea. It was later in 1875 that an American journalist called Henry Stanley sailed around the whole of Lake Victoria. He proved that the Ripon Falls were the source and that Speke had been completely correct in his claim. Several years later, the Ripon Falls were submerged behind the Owen Falls dam a little farther downstream. A monument to Speke can be seen on the bank at Jinja where it is supposed he stood as he realised his important discovery.

A memorial bust of Mahatma Ghandi has been erected on the opposite bank, as he had lived in Uganda for some years and wished for some of his ashes to be spread on the site. The Owen Falls dam was built here in 1954. When you drive towards Jinja, you pass the dam that harnesses the power of the Nile River to produce electricity for Uganda as well as Kenya and Tanzania. My favourite site in Jinja was always the Bugagali Falls and I was saddened when these had to be submerged in 2012 to make room for a second dam. Such was the rising popularity and need for electricity as the country developed.

Over the years, more and more communication masts have been erected in Kampala and its surrounding areas. As Kampala is built on seven hills, these masts are very noticeable, particularly in the area where several television studios are sited. In my second month of being in the school, I visited the Lighthouse studio to make an advertisement to attract more pupils to our school. Mike had arranged for a film crew to come and film our pupils in action. I was already proud of our school and wanted it showcased in the best possible way, so I set up various creative and visually pleasing shots that they could film. The children were confident, happy and good at presentations so they performed well. Later I attended the studio to give a two-minute presentation about Wellspring School. I prepared this carefully and learnt it by heart. When Mike and I returned to view the finished production, we were delighted with it. Over that Christmas period and school holiday, the advertisement was shown more than seventy times across the nation. I experienced my own fifteen minutes of fame! We repeated the exercise the following year but after that our numbers were continually increasing so we no longer found it necessary to advertise in this way.

Modern terrorism showed its evil face in Kampala during the summer of 2010, whilst I was back in England for a few weeks. I was truly horrified and shocked as the stories unfolded on the news and I saw injured Ugandans being helped from bomb wreckage. The terrorists picked sites where both national and Western people would be gathered together to watch the World Cup football matches. The loss of lives in this way was so tragic. Ugandan forces support the fight against Al-Shabab in Somalia and this was an attack against their involvement there. Further attacks in a Kenyan shopping mall and at a university also destroyed the hopes and dreams of many individuals. When you come to identify with a nation and you know and love its people, you are profoundly hurt to see them suffer in this way.

In 2012, the Olympic Games came to London. Once again, I was in England and I enjoyed watching a very good friend carry the Olympic torch through London as well as cheering on cyclist Bradley Wiggins as he raced right through my home town of Molesey. The closing ceremony brought Uganda back onto the world stage in a very exciting way. Ugandan runner Kiprotitch had won the marathon the day before and the medals ceremony was part of the closing ceremony. I stood in front of my television and sang along proudly with the Ugandan national anthem as Kiprotitch received his gold medal. All the world was watching this victory and achievement. I could visualise the red dusty paths he would have run along as a young boy; racing to school, running to collect water, chasing the goats and now, by racing along the roads of London, he had succeeded in the ultimate race.

PART SIX

Viewpoint

Twenty years from now, you will be more disappointed by the things you didn't do than by the things you did do. So throw off the bowlines. Sail away from the safe harbour. Catch the trade winds in your sails. Explore. Dream. Discover.[10]

H. Jackson Brown's mother

The site where Speke identified the source of the River Nile.

---

[10] *P.S. I Love You: When Mom Wrote, She Always Saved the Best for Last*; H. Jackson Brown (1991)

91

Open Spaces

Long before I ever went to Uganda, I had a dream one night that I knew was significant for my future. In this dream, I could see vast vistas of landscape and the words 'Wide Open Spaces'. Not long after, I moved house and noticed a sign as I drove into my road that pointed to the river and 'Open Space'. Although this was very specific, I didn't think that fitted the image of my dream. When I moved to Uganda, the scenery and the words matched together fully. Wherever I went, I was visually impressed by the sky; it was just so open, wide and vast. Clouds drifted across this huge expanse but were so much bigger and more magnificent in shape and form than I had ever seen before. The brightness of the sun lit them with glorious splendour. It was like standing before a beautiful piece of art that constantly changed in shape, colour and direction.

Towards evening when the sun began to set, the colours daubed across the canvas blended through burnt shades of red, orange and yellow until the blacker streaks of the night consumed the whole. During the light of day, the horizon stretching before me seemed to engender hope, expectation and a feeling of great joy.

> *What lies before us and what lies behind us are small matters compared to what lies 'within' us. When we bring what is within us out into the world, miracles happen.*[11]

I felt I had come home. My heart was bursting with love for this nation. The 'wide open spaces' beckoned me to express my own creativity and style in offering what lay within me – my talents and strengths – to enrich and bring hope to these wonderful people who lived in a world of contrasts. I was living within a spacious place. Like David the Psalmist, I could testify that:

---

[11] *Meditations in Wall Street;* Henry Stanley Haskins; W. Morrow & Company (1940)

The LORD brought me out into a spacious place, he rescued me because he delighted in me.

Psalm 18:19

A spacious place still needs boundaries and it is these that provide security and safety. I was free to 'move and have [my] being'[12], but I was able to feel secure in the boundaries that Wellspring provided. I could also agree that:

The boundary lines have fallen for me in pleasant places.

Psalm 16:6

Working at Wellspring, I was given a clear and specific role to fulfil. I had the freedom to develop the school as I thought best but I worked within the safety of a management team that would check, advise or question. This, for me, provided a safe 'wide open space'. Within our senior team, we pursued a policy of honesty and accountability to each other. This is quite ground-breaking as most Ugandans do not like to face confrontation at all, preferring to avoid issues that may bring tension or disagreement. By being honest with each other, we could face difficult issues, work through them together and maintain our good relationships. The success of our work depended on the strength and wholeness of these relationships. The Wisdom of Solomon found in Proverbs 4:23 was our directive:

Above all else, guard your heart, for it is the wellspring of life.

This was a great wise proverb for all of us who worked at Wellspring and indeed for all of us in our human relationships.

In the course of my work and life in Uganda, there were many frustrations that had the potential to become stumbling blocks. If I mulled over these situations in my mind, they would create a negative attitude. At such times, I made a conscious decision to invite the Holy Spirit to change me and bring God's peace and perspective. I saw this as a choice between two alternatives: one being like a dried-up sponge, hard, brittle and not fit for purpose; the other being like a soft sponge soaked in water, functioning as designed. Such a sponge, or chosen reaction, would then be flexible and able to benefit all. When tempted

---

[12] Acts 17:28

to justify my complaint to myself and meditate on it, a verse in Isaiah encouraged me to take a better path:

> *God is your teacher ... if you wander from the right path, either to the right or to the left, you will hear a voice behind you saying, "You should go this way. Here is the right way."*

Isaiah 30:21 (ERV)

The right path always proved beneficial to me personally as well as in my work.

Working within a Christian organisation, you tend to participate in the same church, social group and community activities. This can result in an intensity between people where apparent favouritism or special privileges can bring about resentments. Misunderstandings and problems then follow and individuals can be hurt. I found a healthy and open attitude prevailed through Wellspring as an organisation. In guarding my own heart, there were times when I needed to apologise for harsh words or poor attitudes that I had expressed in my work context. This way of dealing with conflict between us enabled us to move forward with a purity in thought, word and deed.

I believe God honours the choices and decisions we make in our individual family life. I have full respect and admiration for the example given by the Wellspring directors, Herbert and Eve. Through their strong marriage, happy family life and their extended family lifestyle, many are blessed and welcomed into their home. Both Herbert and Eve are well educated and qualified with numerous gifts between them. They have the potential to be employed in high government posts or a large business. Instead, they have chosen to serve the community around them in a humble and self-sacrificing way. Their grace and generosity to others is amazing and they are able to forgive even when friends disappoint them or cause hurt. I believe it is through the wellspring of their hearts that God chooses to bless, honour and reward the work carried out through the Wellspring partnership.

Umbrellas Up

There are two wet seasons during the year in Uganda. Throughout these months, the rain can attack like a tropical storm with thunder, lightning and a powerful wind. Ugandans hate the rain because they connect it with mosquitoes breeding and the onslaught of malaria. Also, for many families living in makeshift housing, the ground becomes thick mud and the rain washes through their small homes, leaving filth and destruction. If people are caught out in the rain, they will huddle under any shelter available and the side roads suddenly appear deserted. Staff arrive late to work and appointments are often delayed until the rain is over. Very few people have their own transport so they walk to work or church. Local roads are unmade roads, where the rain and mud splashes over your legs and trousers.

In my first few weeks, I had no transport so I walked to work each day. Sometimes I needed to wash my feet and legs when I arrived, to clean off the mud and marks. Umbrellas are a luxury, so my teachers used small black plastic bags to wrap round their hair to protect their styles. Everyone looks for cover if they are vulnerable to being drenched, splashed by dirt or, worse, slipping right over into the muddy earth.

The right covering provided the best protection and this is true in a practical way as well as spiritually. We have not been made to work in isolation. We need people around us to hold us accountable, provide encouragement and support us in our mission. When I moved to Uganda, I did not do this in isolation. Being single and on my own, I knew I might face unique difficulties. As a member of a local community church based in Molesey, I knew I had the 'spiritual covering' of the church leadership. This group of people knew me well, my strengths and my weaknesses. They had stood alongside me through good and bad times. They knew that I was taking a risk and that past poor mental health could resurface in a different environment and culture. They believed, however, that through God I had a calling to fulfil in Africa. They had encouraged me in pursuing this dream and would support me in any way they could as I stepped into fulfilling it. I knew that if I faced any difficulties, they would offer good, honest advice and wisdom.

When you step into a vastly different culture from your own, there can be pressures and stresses put upon you. You are aware of adverse spiritual forces such as demonic powers, witchcraft traditions and spirits that can affect individuals and whole communities. You need to be assured that your very soul and inner being is under protection. I felt safe and secure the whole time I was in Uganda. I was confident in the 'spiritual umbrella' that covered me in every situation I faced and I was able to step out in a new, more powerful spiritual authority as a result.

Healing Happens

When you live in a country that has no national health provision, you become so grateful for what we have through our National Health Service in Britain. I have watched many families struggle to provide even the most basic of healthcare. When you can hardly afford to clothe, feed and educate your children, emergency costs prove impossible. Many times, the least favourable option is taken due to financial constraints. If you are able to pay more, you can expect better medical care.

Wellspring has a health centre which offers twenty-four-hour care to the community. The staff are committed, cheerful and hard-working. They deal with emergencies in a calm and dedicated manner. I recall the morning when several cars drove very quickly into the forecourt by our school and health centre. Rushing outside, I learned there had been a serious accident at a nearby factory and that many people were needing attention. Some of the injured were unconscious and were carried from cars. Others were helped into wheelchairs.

The whole Wellspring team went into action, alongside the medical staff. We made all our conference accommodation available once the beds were all taken at the health centre. I ran to my home next door to retrieve additional mattresses. The more urgent cases were rushed in to be dealt with first. In all, there were about fifty women suffering shock, pain or injury. It transpired that a large fan had crashed suddenly from the ceiling onto the people working below. This sudden noise and disruption caused a panic as people suspected that a bomb had exploded. Everybody had rushed immediately to the exit door, crushing some in the mayhem that followed. Most of them had lost their shoes in the process.

Our medical staff performed wonderfully and by that afternoon each person had received treatment and was able to rest on the emergency bedding we had provided. Fortunately, only a small number needed to remain under care and supervision overnight: the others had suffered only minor cuts and injuries.

I felt a concern for these women and for how the shock they had experienced might damage them in future. It was a great privilege later in the day to enter every ward and room where the ladies were resting and offer to pray with them. They welcomed this suggestion and lay peacefully while I thanked God for a safe recovery, blessed them in the name of Jesus and prayed against any emotional or mental trauma as a result of this experience. For the few that were in the ward and unable to speak, I was able to pray quietly by their bedsides. That evening, those who could return home were collected by bus to return to the factory to collect their bags and possessions. I stood by the entrance to the bus to say goodbye to each one. Many were smiling and cheerful by now and very grateful for the care they had received. Few of them had their shoes and one older lady was limping badly towards the bus steps. I was able to remove mine and pass them to her. It was a special and humbling moment.

The following day, we received messages from the factory directors congratulating and appreciating us for the care we had shown their staff throughout this ordeal. The factory produces well-known hair accessories for weaving and plaiting so the incident had been covered by the national television and newspapers. We felt proud that our facilities had been able to provide such good service for this incident.

One Sunday morning, we were told about a situation a family in our church was facing. Their firstborn son and only child was suffering greatly and had been ever since his birth. He had an irritating skin complaint that completely covered his body. Now, just about eighteen months old, he cried constantly from the itching and distress this caused him. Close friends had been praying for some relief but the situation was not improving. We were asked as a church family to pray and fast over the coming week in order to see a breakthrough. The pressure was beginning to cause the parents to despair. I committed to praying for this young boy and during the week, I visited the family so I could be in their home and pray with them. We were thrilled as a church to see a real improvement fairly soon and, ultimately, a complete healing. The lad turned from an unhappy sick child into a cheerful and lively boy. The parents were overjoyed to begin a happy and more normal family life.

On another occasion, I spoke at church about stepping beyond the veil, from death and into the resurrection life of Jesus. I had hung a large red cloth at the front which we tore down to represent the veil in the temple. Behind it were words on cards representing all the situations in life that trouble us, such as fear, anger, sickness, poverty, loss of hope, anxiety. I had prepared some small pieces of fabric to represent the veil and I encouraged people to come forward and take one of these from a basket. I explained that I had no knowledge of their need but they knew it and God did too. They could use the fabric and tear it themselves as a symbol of the area in their lives from which they wanted to break free. There was a huge response as people confronted situations and looked to God to bring healing. At this time, the wife of one of our leaders was suffering from a debilitating illness. She responded to this word and opened her heart and body to receive healing. The following Sunday, she came to the front and told everyone how she had seen a massive improvement in her health. We continued to meet and pray with her, believing that a complete healing would be fulfilled for her and in due time, this actually happened.

I found myself being called on to pray with people suffering from illness on several occasions. One of our young men had a very unfortunate condition and several operations had not rectified it. For several years, we supported him in love and prayer, wanting to see him healed. When I returned to England, I learnt that his difficult malfunction had been completely healed. Then, when I visited Uganda again, I saw a totally different person. He was now well, happy and confident in himself. He has developed into a very reliable member of the church, working with the young people and being a blessing to all.

Of course, we also faced disappointment when we prayed earnestly for situations that did not seem to change for the better or in the way we imagined. Despite this, we continued to be active and positive in believing in the power of a miraculous and supernatural God. We continued to offer situations to him still, allowing him the opportunity to demonstrate his power. As C.S. Lewis put it:

A miracle is interference with nature by supernatural power.[13]

Like him, we too wanted to see such miracles.

---

[13] *Miracles: A Preliminary Study;* C.S. Lewis (1947)

Pit Stops

When I first began considering a move to work in Uganda, the risk element was discussed with my church leaders and the directors of Wellspring. There was no guarantee that living in another culture and facing different problems would not prove too stressful and lead to poor mental health, which I had experienced before. We were all in agreement that this was the right path ahead of me but we built in safety measures in case they were necessary at any given time. This involved regular communication with key friends and at least one visit from England each year of a pastoral type. For a single person, it is harder to embark on a move to another country than for someone with a partner and family. Tensions and pressures of living in a different culture and working in a Christian organisation have to be worked through without the help of a close partner who can support, advise or even challenge your perspectives. To maintain good mental and emotional health requires a mature approach to working relationships and a healthy attitude to money. It is usually within these two areas that conflicts arise and sadly lead to fractured relationships, mistrust, jealousy or resentment. This leads inevitably to burnout, division and disillusionment.

I am very grateful for the years I have enjoyed being part of a church community in Molesey, where honesty, generosity, forgiveness and grace are the hallmarks of our working together. These strong roots enabled me to respond to challenges in a positive manner that maintained peace and harmony throughout my time in Uganda.

It is easy to write about the successes and satisfaction of mission work abroad and the adventures associated with it but sometimes there is another story to tell of the cost involved. Over the last thirty or more years, I have had a few episodes of serious depression. This could occur following a period of acute stress through work or personal difficulties but at other times I worked through high-pressured times with ease. Sometimes there would be no obvious cause for why I entered a low period. If I were asked to identify what had been the trigger, I had no answer. It happened because it happened. People who have had no experience of depression themselves find it very hard to understand its causes, symptoms and difficulties.

Depression is an illness and is not caused by a character weakness. It brings physical discomfort and a general sense of unwellness. It can also produce psychological problems but my difficulties are of a physical nature. For me, personally, symptoms can include:

- poor coordination, resulting in items being dropped or scattered;
- intolerance of sudden and loud noises;
- very slow movements, like walking through thick mud;
- jittery and shaky feeling in the body;
- a feeling of heaviness, weighing down the body and making any small task seem daunting;
- a desire to sleep due to fatigue, which is completely different from tiredness;
- difficulty in engaging in conversation, lack of emotional energy to interact as usual;
- a tendency to withdraw from social situations where expectations can't be met;
- anxiety in being among a large group of people who may not understand how you feel;
- particular difficulty in the first part of the day. As the day progresses, symptoms can improve but not in a lasting way.

Improvement in the evening can become a pressure if friends don't understand depression. Seeing you engage and interact in a usual manner, they can expect you to continue this way. The morning after can be completely different, yet it is hard to explain that. Those temporary evening improvements are appreciated but do not indicate an immediate path of wellness. As a person who fulfils commitments and responsibilities faithfully, I find it hard being unable to meet an obligation, whether it is a social or a work commitment. Fortunately, the general pattern is that I remain well for a year or so and the problems are forgotten whilst I pursue activities and adventures with enthusiasm and energy.

During my years in Uganda, I was very fortunate as on the whole I stayed well and remained healthy. However, there were a few times when I felt poorly and knew it was not caused by a virus, bug or sickness. At Wellspring, I was very fortunate in having Eve as my immediate line manager. She never put any pressure on me to explain myself. I would tell her I was not feeling too well and that I would manage this by approaching my work more slowly and allowing some space. She completely trusted me in this and usually after two or three days with this approach, I was back to full strength. If not, we just agreed together that I would take a couple of days off to rest. There was only one occasion on which I was not picking up following a parasite in my system and fatigue seemed to have set in. Then I needed a longer break and I arranged an extended visit back to England, where I soon returned to full health. As I had been away for five years at this time, it seemed good practice (in hindsight) to plan a longer break at such a point in an overseas mission.

I have to be realistic and know that if I overstretch myself, there may be unfortunate consequences, but generally I aim to pace myself and allow space between busy, demanding periods. However, I am not prepared to live a cosseted lifestyle just to protect myself. Life is for living fully within realistic and appropriate aims. I am very grateful for the physical health and energy I enjoy and appreciate all the opportunities I have had. I live with an awareness that I may face a time of depression in the future that could last two days, two weeks or even, at worst, two months. It will pass though, and during it I remain thankful for good physical health, home and the understanding of family and friends.

Depression, just like any other illness, has to be managed through medication, understanding and a lifestyle that pays respect to the whole person in mind, body and spirit. I have not allowed it to hinder or limit what I believe I am in a unique position to offer: education in Africa. My passion for children, schools and people in general will continue to be expressed in Uganda and elsewhere.

Depression does not bring a dead end to destiny!

The following is a piece of writing I expressed during a time of depression, yet I was hopeful and looking forward to the time when it would be over.

> *Lord, I am so flat*
> *Like a run-out battery*
> *No energy*
> *No get up and go*
> *No light or life*

Dragging steps
Muffled head
Wobbly legs.
It has happened again.
It will pass I know
But 'til it does
I'm stuck in limbo
Waiting, crouching low
Stepping cautiously.

It's spring out there
It's a sunny day
Leaves are in bud
They're on their way
They won't come late
Or not too soon.
But one day I will look
And the bud will have bloomed
No longer barren
The tree will sing its refrain
A glorious new season
Comes in fullness again.

The cycle never fails.
Life always bursts out free.
So I'll let that sun shine on
Give it permission
To warmly embrace me.
Stirring up my inner hope
I will look forward
Take a look outside
Believing renewal has begun.
I always know that
Soon I will burst through
I will be crowned anew.

But when you send out your life-giving breath, things come alive,
and the world is like new again.

Psalm 104:30

Climbing Mountains

Norman Barnes, the founder and former director of the charity Links International, spoke at our church many years ago. He challenged us to climb a mountain that stood metaphorically in our path. If you wanted to succeed in climbing it, it would be far better to try to fail than stay near the safety of its base, never knowing if you could have made the ascent and reached the top. It can be too easy to let our fears and struggles stop us from taking risks and prevent us from ever realising our potential. For me personally, my move to Uganda was a risk but I wanted to climb that mountain placed before me. What I saw, learnt and experienced changed my life considerably. I felt I had truly stepped into my destiny.

There is a unique calling for each one of us to discover and embrace, but it is not automatically guaranteed for us. It depends on the choices we make throughout our lives. As I put my trust in God, he wove all the bad and the good together into one complete picture. Our past failures do not have to dictate our future. Failure is not a full-stop with God.

A taxi in Kampala had the slogan, 'No condition is permanent.' Failure is not permanent either. It is a season that can lead us on to better and more fulfilling adventures. I have always appreciated the seasons we enjoy in Britain. Living in a constant temperature in Uganda gave no shades of colour or changing flora and I missed the rhythm of our seasons. New seasons can bring excitement and motivation to move out of the usual and expected, and step into new opportunities and challenges.

Sir Francis Drake carried out a circumnavigation of the world in his single expedition which lasted from 1577 to 1580. He was part of a very ordinary but devoutly religious family. His father was a Protestant preacher and the Protestant faith came to represent one of the most important aspects of Drake's life. When he was on board ship, sailing around the world, he led services twice a day for the crew. On a retreat once, I was introduced to a poem that is attributed to Sir Francis Drake and I find it most inspiring:

Disturb us, Lord, when
We are too well pleased with ourselves,
When our dreams have come true
Because we have dreamed too little,
When we arrived safely
Because we sailed too close to the shore.

Disturb us, Lord, when
With the abundance of things we possess
We have lost our thirst
For the water of life;
Having fallen in love with life,
We have ceased to dream of eternity
And in our efforts to build a new earth,
We have allowed our vision
Of the new Heaven to dim.

Disturb us, Lord, to dare more boldly,
To venture on wider seas
Where storms will show your mastery;
Where losing sight of land,
We shall find the stars.
We ask you to push back
The horizons of our hopes;
And to push into the future
In strength, courage, hope and love.

I love the phrase 'the horizons of our hopes'. We all have hopes for ourselves and for others. Hope is such a happy and positive word. It looks to the future with anticipation and faith and believes the best in all things.

Horizons can limit our view and perspective. But we can ask God to push back those horizons so we see the bigger picture unfold before us. The 'wide open spaces' of opportunity are there waiting for us to grasp. Sometimes we need to be stirred to get out of the safe boat and walk on the water and over the horizon.

Destiny is there for those who dare to dream, who don't give up, who step through failure and who then enter their promised land.

PART SEVEN

No Stopping

You must have the courage to accept the fluidity of elements that happen in development. Every development, every departure, means leaving something behind.[14]

Daniel Barenboim

Leaving someone behind.

---

[14] *Parallels and Paradoxes;* Daniel Barenboim and Edward W. Said

Moving Forward

During my teaching career in England, I undertook a two-year course: the National Professional Qualification for head teachers, known as the NPQH. Whilst leading Wellspring School, I realized a similar course would be beneficial in Africa as there was no such training available for head teachers or potential head teachers. I decided to write and develop material based on my NPQH studies, adapting them to be relevant to circumstances in Africa. The first cohort I ran at Wellspring had fifteen attendees and ran for a week. I made my course very different from the ones run by the local education office: the traditional lecture-type presentation was replaced with interaction, analysis, data interpretation, role play and group presentations. A range of topics included: Vision, Managing Change, The Interview Process and School Development Plans. I received an email recently from Peter, who had been on the course and now runs his own school near Kampala. In it he expressed his appreciation for this course and also the amount he had learnt from working alongside me in the Wellspring School, where for a time he was the head teacher while I acted as his mentor and overseer.

Throughout my life's work in education, I have been in contact with over 5000 children and worked alongside countless adults. In my role as an educator, I have always pictured an image of a wheel. As a class teacher for many years, I was at the hub of that wheel working with an average of thirty pupils. As a head teacher in both Surrey and Uganda, I was responsible for more than three hundred pupils in each school I led. This seemed like the wheel spokes branching out into a wider sphere of influence. In running my course in management and leadership, I hoped to influence the teaching and learning for thousands of pupils. The heads who attended would be like the outer rim of the wheel who would circulate within many schools, spreading and sharing good practice.

As I continue to travel to Uganda and other parts of Africa, I intend to deliver and develop this course further. I want my legacy to be a living one, illustrated in the lives of the children and educators I have been privileged to help. My hope is that they will fulfil their dreams and aspire to greater heights in all they want to achieve.

Send Me

I have lived back in England for four years now and many people have wondered why I returned instead of continuing what I was doing in Uganda. The book of Ecclesiastes in the Old Testament teaches that there is a right time for everything in our lives. I could have easily remained longer for my own enjoyment but was clear in my own mind and heart that I had accomplished what I had been asked to do eight years earlier. The school was well established, numbers were high, standards were good and the top class was performing well year-on-year in their final leaving exams. The staff were working with clear objectives, organised systems, good teamwork and strong motivation. They were being led now by a Ugandan head teacher, and I was just simply overseeing this. I had worked my way out of a job! This had always been the aim.

Knowing when to step back or down is crucial. The decision to go to Uganda was not all about my own fulfilment and ministry. It was to serve, encourage and establish others. I knew clearly when I began that I would know when my task was completed. There is a time to remain and a time to leave. From a personal point of view, I was aware of age creeping up on myself and my three sisters. During my time in Uganda, two of my sisters had been ill with cancer and undergone surgery. I wanted to be able to spend more time with them and their families. They had supported me lovingly in my moving away and I had been absent from many special family events and celebrations. Now I could be a part of that family life again.

I returned in 2013 and enjoyed settling back into my home and familiar surroundings. My life for nearly eight years had been so different that at first it felt as though I had died and come back to life. Not because life was any better or happier here, as I had been completely happy in Uganda. It was just the experience of adjusting and enjoying all the conveniences, luxuries and time-saving devices that surround our Western lifestyle. On short visits back, I had dipped into this way of life but now I was fully engaged again with the fast pace of living in England. At times in Uganda, I had felt quite cut off from everyone back in England and wished for more communication from friends. Seeing the busy-ness of life for everyone here, I understood better how I could slip easily from people's minds.

Once I had settled into home, bought a car and generally sorted out all the practical aspects of being a permanent resident again, I began to re-engage in local and church activities. Every year I travel at least once to Uganda or another African country where I give training for teachers and head teachers. Whilst living in Uganda, I wrote the previously mentioned course to train head teachers within Africa in management and leadership skills. I have led this at Wellspring and also in Mukono, a nearby area where a group of teachers requested the course. I have worked also with Links International to produce and present teaching materials for primary pupils in Africa about healthy living. We are currently working to develop this material for schools in more rural areas where different problems arise and resources are limited.

I was drawn recently to read the story of the prophet Joshua in the Bible. He had achieved so much in his lifetime but as he got older, it seemed there was no time to sit back and settle down to a quiet life. In Joshua 13:1-5, God speaks to him and says:

> *Joshua, you have grown old, <u>but</u> there is still much land for you to take control of.*[15]

He then proceeds to point out the opportunities and challenges still ahead of Joshua:

> *You have not yet...*
>
> *You must still go as far...*
>
> *You must still defeat...*
>
> *You must still go north...*
>
> *And also there is the area of...*

It is not until much later in Joshua 23:1 that we read:

> *Joshua became <u>very</u> old.*[16]

I am encouraged, motivated and challenged by these words. I want to be like Joshua and have opportunities and challenges ahead of me

---

[15] ERV, emphasis added
[16] ERV, emphasis added

always. I want to use my skills, experience and energy in further developing education in Africa and trust that God will continue to use me in helping many more young people achieve their potential.

Epilogue

You are a missionary woman.

You will be going abroad helping and changing schools.

Other schools will ask for assistance and you will be moving on to help these too.

You will also be training head teachers as well as working alongside women.

You will continue to do this into your old age.

You will live a long life.

This is the prophecy that predicted a new direction in my life. Nearly every statement in it has become a reality. Now, I am looking forward to living and enjoying that long life.

What Shall I Read Next?

All By Grace
Jim Cockburn
ISBN 978-1-911086-71-0

Jim Cockburn spent 37 years of his life in teaching and 21 years as the headteacher of a comprehensive school in north-east England, a career that he loved. As Jim sought to apply Christian principles to the many challenging situations he encountered as a headteacher, he regularly experienced God's grace and strength. His goal in every situation was to live out the Christian life in a practical way and to share the love of Jesus with others. This book, in which Jim tells his story and reflects on the significance of events and decisions made, will be of great interest to all Christians in education.

Where Love Leads You
Ruth Deeth
ISBN 978-1-907509-39-1

When an ordinary young woman gives her life into the hands of Jesus, extraordinary things begin to happen. Suddenly she finds herself taken away from her familiar Western culture to serve a nomadic tribe living in the hills and plains of Amudat, completely oblivious of the Kenya/Uganda border. Ruth faces great challenges in adapting to the culture of the people she wants to introduce to Jesus. As she lives with the local people, Ruth encounters their diet of cow's blood and milk and their traditional customs and religious sacrifices. In trying to provide medical care, she faces the obstacles of superstitious beliefs and tribal politics. After a government coup in Uganda she is thrown into jail. However, each of Ruth's challenges gives her an opportunity to express the love of Christ to the people around her. It is only after she has left East Africa that she discovers the lasting impact Jesus has made through her – and sometimes in spite of her...